RAW
GARDEN

over
100
healthy & fresh
raw
recipes

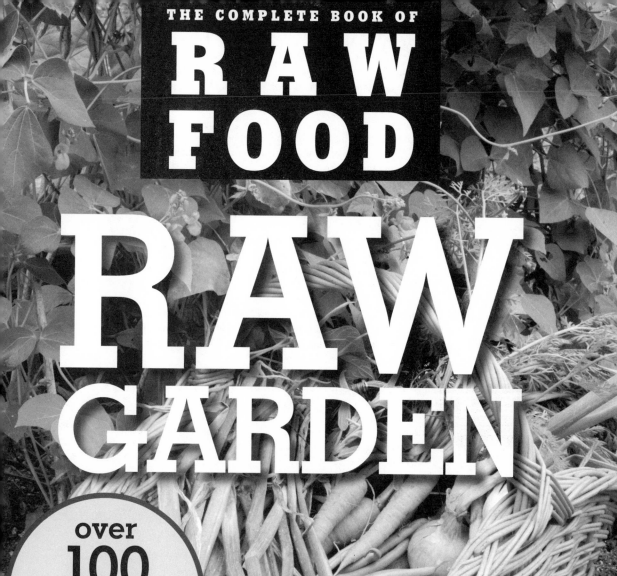

THE COMPLETE BOOK OF

RAW FOOD

RAW GARDEN

over **100** healthy & fresh raw recipes

Lisa Montgomery

hatherleigh

Hatherleigh Press is committed to preserving and protecting the natural resources of the Earth. Environmentally responsible and sustainable practices are embraced within the company's mission statement.

Hatherleigh Press is a member of the Publishers Earth Alliance, committed to preserving and protecting the natural resources of the planet while developing a sustainable business model for the book publishing industry.

This book was edited in the village of Hobart, New York. Hobart is a community that has embraced books and publishing as a component of its livelihood. There are several unique bookstores in the village. For more information, please visit www.hobartbookvillage.com.

Library of Congress Cataloging-in-Publication Data is available.
ISBN: 978-1-57826-385-1

Raw Garden is available for bulk purchase, special promotions, and premiums. For information on reselling and special purchase opportunities, call 1-800-528-2550 and ask for the Special Sales Manager.

Cover design by DCDesign
Interior design by DCDesign

10 9 8 7 6 5 4 3 2 1
Printed in the United States

This book is dedicated in memory of my Mom, Carol Jane Hecht
Montgomery. My Mom died so I could live. She is my hero.
APRIL 19, 1924–MAY 16, 2010

— ✸ —

*"You gain strength, courage and confidence by every
experience in which you really stop to look fear in the face.
You must do the thing you think you cannot do."*
—ELEANOR ROOSEVELT

I want to thank everyone who made *Raw Garden* possible.
Thank you for blessing my life.

CONTENTS

INTRODUCTION

When I first changed my diet and started this healthy food journey sixteen years ago, I never could have guessed that I would also end up with a full-fledged heirloom organic garden, berry plants, fruit trees, bees, and chickens. Who knew that changing my diet and lifestyle could lead me to such a huge shift?

My first book, *Raw Inspiration*, was the beginner book to a healthy, "living dynamically" lifestyle, whereas *Raw Garden* is a bit more advanced, since it takes you to the next level of a raw lifestyle. In *Raw Inspiration*, I showed you how to begin living dynamically in all areas of your life. In *Raw Garden*, I will give you the tools to live your healthiest lifestyle by growing your own food.

As always, I will give you the uncomplicated straight facts on how to grow your food. Just like you, I am juggling many balls and have more demands on my time than hours in the day. So I, too, understand that any lifestyle change must be quick and easy, which is what you will find in the following pages.

By creating your own raw garden, you not only have the opportunity to enjoy fresh, home-grown meals every day, but you are also empowered as you learn to take control of your health, your life, and your food. There is a unique excitement in planning your own garden and picking what you are going to grow each year. Personally, I prefer to grow my favorites, but I also love trying new varieties as well.

In today's world, most of us are struggling with limited time and resources, making it seem even more challenging to make healthy changes in our lives.

Many people are without work, and those who are lucky enough to have jobs are working longer hours than ever before, which can put a strain on your family life. By the time you get home from work, you are already exhausted and still have to put food on the table, help the kids with their homework, and clean the house. With all of these responsibilities, how can I possibly be asking you to grow your own food? I know it may seem impossible now, but with my easy tips, you will soon discover that keeping a raw garden is not only possible, but it is also healthy and fun. Rather than opening up a package of chemical-laden food, you will be preparing fresh, organic meals to nourish you and your family. Plus, having a raw garden is something that you can do together as a family. Working in the soil is very grounding and stress-releasing. Heck, I don't know about you, but we used to play in the dirt pile as kids, and, now, with a garden, you get to play in the dirt pile together as a family.

Keeping a garden together will also encourage your family to share quality time during meals. Unfortunately, a lot of families no longer have family dinners, because the parents work late hours, and the kids are involved in many different activities. Yet by planning, planting, maintaining, and harvesting your garden together, your family can communicate with each other and remain bonded. Not only will your family be healthier emotionally, but you will also be healthier physically, because you will be eating better. Growing your own food may also inspire your family to create new recipes to use what you harvest, and *Raw Garden* will provide lots of healthy recipes for you to try as well.

In the years since I have started raw gardening, I have discovered a stronger connection with the land and the nourishment that it provides through my harvest. Once the weather breaks in the spring and the days grow longer, I am so content with being in my garden that you just cannot keep me indoors. Having chickens even keeps me out in the yard year-round. During the cold winter months, I still walk out to my garden and enjoy viewing it, even when it is covered in snow. I take a daily stroll to visit my bees, snuggled down in their hives for the winter. They hate the cold, but, luckily, it will stay nice and warm in the center of their hives. The chickens are always out in their yard, wondering what tasty treat I will be bringing them, while my dogs Charlie and Riley follow me as I pick up wood to be used as kindling for the fireplace. I cannot think of a happier, more peaceful place on the face of the earth than my home and my backyard. So, if for no other reason, having a raw garden will fill your heart with peace and joy, making it worth every penny that you spend and every moment of time that you enjoy planning it, tending to it, or harvesting it.

Until you begin your own raw garden, you will not believe how much fulfillment that you can gain from such a lifestyle. You owe it to yourself to throw away the excuses and make some positive changes for you and your family. I, too, understand how difficult it can be to maintain healthy living. I have two full-time jobs: one as a packaging sales representative, and another promoting healthy living through raw potlucks, speaking, demoing, and book writing. I recently faced a personal tragedy when my beloved Mom passed away after almost dying eleven times in the last two-and-a-half years, which required me to continuously travel to my parents' house and the hospital. After my Mom's passing, there have also been challenges with my eighty-seven-year-old dad and all that that encompasses. Despite all of this, I still fit in my exercise and my own well-being. If I can do all of this and live this lifestyle, so can you. To be honest, I firmly believe that if I did not live such a healthy lifestyle, I would have cracked under the pressure. If I did not take care of myself emotionally, physically, and spiritually, I would never have survived all of the turmoil that this year has presented. Although it may seem like a lot of work, I am worth it, and you are, too. Please take back control of the emotional, physical, and spiritual well-being of you and your family. Start today by planting the seeds of your raw garden, so you can "live dynamically."

Because I have been blessed to take raw cooking classes for the past ten years with raw chefs and teachers on both coasts, I am able to bring you some of my favorite recipes that I have learned. Before I started preparing healthy food, I had been taking cooking classes at local restaurants and high schools (not to mention standing by my Mom in the kitchen as a toddler). My Mom could have easily blown me off when I wanted to learn, because it would have been easier to just do it herself, but she took the time to teach all of my three siblings and me to cook. My Mom did not know how to cook when she got married, so she wanted to make sure we were never in that position. Ironically, for a woman who did not know how to cook when she got out of college and got married, she ended up being one of the best cooks whom I have ever known. No one put more love into their food than my Mom. This book is dedicated to my Mom, Carol Jane Hecht Montgomery, as she passed on May 16, 2010, at the age of eighty-six.

HOW TO GET STARTED

PLANNING YOUR GARDEN

The first step in beginning a raw garden is to plan out what you will plant. This should be based on how much space you have available for planting, what you like, the length of your planting season, and how many people whom you need to feed out of your garden.

For example, I have room in my back lawn for eight raised beds, each holding four plants, which totals thirty-two plants. Since I only have room for thirty-two plants in my raised bed, I have to decide what I will be planting and where. I usually plant one bed each (four plants) of squash, peppers, cucumbers (cucumbers can be replanted during the season, so you can harvest all season), and eggplant. In the remaining four beds, I plant a variety of tomato plants (from cherry tomatoes to beef-steak). In the middle of my back lawn, I have a flower bed where I grow additional tomato plants and, this year, I will plant watermelons among the peonies (this will be my first attempt at growing watermelon, and I can hardly wait to see how they do).

Once you have determined what you are going to plant, you will need to order your seeds. Below are a few of my favorite seed catalogs:

BAKER CREEK HEIRLOOM SEEDS (MANSFIELD, MO)

www.rareseeds.com

(417) 924-8917

Baker Creek Heirloom carries 1,400 heirloom seeds that are all non-hybrid and non-GMO seeds.

COMSTOCK SEEDS (WETHERSFIELD, CT)

www.comstockfere.com

(860) 571-6590

Comstock is a 200-year old company. One major advantage of ordering from them is that they carry watercress seeds and native heirloom organic seeds.

HIGH MOWING ORGANIC SEEDS (WOLCOTT, VT)

www.highmowingseeds.com

(802) 472-6174

This company carries organic seeds.

Seed Savers Exchange (Deborah, IA)

www.seedsavers.org

(563) 382-5990

This company carries heirloom seeds.

Mt. Rose Herbs (Eugene, OR)

www.mountainroseherbs.com

(800) 879-3337

Mt. Rose Herbs carries a wonderful selection of herb seeds (medicinal and edible).

Horizon Herbs (Williams, OR)

www.horizonherbs.com

(541) 846-6704

This is another company with a wonderful selection of herb seeds (medicinal and edible).

Gardener's Supply (Burlington, VT)

www.gardeners.com

(800) 427-3363

Gardener's Supply provides a selection of innovative tools, supplies, and gardening advice from compost to harvest.

EMERGENCY PREPAREDNESS

Over the last several years, I have been reading about food shortages and attempts by large GMO (genetically-modified) seed corporations to take over our food supply. Because of this, I always order extra seeds for planting and sprouting in case of an emergency. This way, I will be able to feed myself for the next few years if it ever becomes necessary. I also stock extra nuts (such as raw almonds, cashews, and walnuts) and seeds (like sunflower and pumpkin) in case our food supply is ever cut off. I have even stockpiled emergency supplies such as extra batteries, light bulbs, candles, oil lamps, wood (for burning in my fireplace), matches, vitamins, paper goods, pet food, cleaning supplies, and cases of drinking water. I must admit that I have even stock-piled extra make-up. What can I say, I am a girl.

I pray to God that I will never have to use my stock-pile of supplies, but at least I know that I am now prepared in case of an emergency. I have shared with you a few of my ideas in the hope that they will inspire you to think about what *you* would do in an emergency and to devise a plan for how you would take care of your family.

In addition to emergency supplies, you should also have a list of emergency contacts. It can also be very helpful to have an emergency plan with local friends or your community, so you all know how you will pull your resources and talents if necessary. I even printed out a list of e-mail addresses of friends, family, and neighbors, so I have a hard copy in case my computer crashes, along with a printed list of any important phone numbers and addresses stored in my cell phone.

HELPFUL GARDENING TOOLS

After you have ordered your seeds, you can begin researching some additional equipment to help you maintain an optimal raw garden. While many of these are not necessary to maintain a garden, you may find specific equipment to be particularly helpful in making your garden the best that it can be.

Accelerated Propagation Starters (APS)–I use the APS trays and premixed soil to start my seeds; they are re-useable and really work. The APS comes with directions, which are easy to follow. I like easy-to-follow directions. Tomato, pepper, and eggplant seeds should be started in your APS trays twelve weeks before you plant them outside, which should always be done after your last frost. Squash seeds can be started four weeks before your last frost.

Tomatoes grown in APS trays. Photo courtesy of Gardener's Supply Company.

Heating Pads–I also use heating pads and place them under my seed starter trays. The heating pads help the seedlings to grow better.

Three-Tier SunLite® Grow Lights–I use these lights (available at Gardener's Supply) to start my seeds in early spring, and I also leave them up all year round. You can first start your seeds in your APS and then place them under the grow lights. One of the neatest things is checking your baby plants each day to watch them burst through the soil and continue to grow. Once the plants are tall enough, you would then thin them, replant in bigger pots, and place them under the grow lights. The seed packets should provide the ideal height to thin each of the seeds. While it is ideal to replant when your seedlings are thicker and shorter, you can still salvage them if you wait a bit longer. This past year, I was extraordinarily busy and replanted my seedlings late when they were already pretty tall and gangly, but once they got outside in the dirt and sunshine, they still thrived.

Cold Frame and Cover–I plant an assortment of greens in my cold frame (available at Gardener's Supply) to protect them over the winter months. Last winter, it snowed more than usual, and when the snow melted and I was finally able to take the cover off, I found my greens had survived through the winter. It is so cool to go out and just cut your greens fresh from your cold frame every day. You will hear me say many times that having a garden is like having Christmas every day, because you always have the gift of fresh food right in your own backyard, and the cold frame helps you to enjoy this all year round. If you use a cold frame, be careful not to leave it open for a prolonged period. I made that mistake this past summer. My greens were beautiful, so I took off the cover and

went to the shore for a long weekend. When I came home, I found that all of my greens had been nibbled off down to the nubs by the local wildlife. I guess the bunnies, squirrels, and birds thought those greens were pretty good, too. This year, I also covered the soil with straw and chicken manure from my very own chickens for nourishment and added protection from the cold (chicken manure is one of the best fertilizers).

I use my cold frame to grow my greens all year long, except for in the winter when there is so much snow that my cold frame is buried.

Fast-start greenhouse. Photo courtesy of Gardener's Supply Company.

Fast-Start Greenhouse–I use my fast-start greenhouse from Gardener's Supply to move the baby plants out to the greenhouse once the weather warms a little, but before it is time to plant them in the soil. I do not have any electricity in the greenhouse, so it works solely on natural sunlight. I line up the baby plants on the shelves in the greenhouse and then use the bottom, which is soil, to plant greens, micro greens, red beets, carrots, and radishes.

Tomato Teepees–Normally in my area (the northwest suburbs of Philadelphia, PA), you can safely plant free of frost after Mother's Day or mid-May. If you rush the season, however, you can plant earlier using teepees. The Tomato Teepees are made of plastic and are filled with water to protect the plants. While I used teepees and rushed the season last year, I think I will wait this year, because I had trouble with the tents falling over and crushing the plants.

Tubtrugs–These are available at Gardener's Supply. You do not have to buy these, but I found them to be very helpful. Tubtrugs are plastic tubs with handles that come in pretty, vibrant colors (I am a girl; what can I say: I love color). These tubs are great for mixing and moistening soil when you start your seedlings or replant. They are also great for hauling when you harvest. Frankly, you will end up finding them very useful even if you do not use them for gardening. The good news is they are pretty indestructible, but do not run out and buy some just to see what it will take to destroy them.

Compost Tumbler–I have a compost tumbler for my composting (for the scraps I don't give my chickens). I like the fact that I can throw the compost material into the tumbler and turn it every day. It is simple and easy to use.

FINDING EQUIPMENT

Much of the equipment discussed in this section can be found at various retailers, but I have had the best experience with Gardener's Supply, an employee-owned company. I love their products, and their customer service is excellent. They have always taken good care of me as a customer, and that is very important to me. Plus, they take the time to answer all of my questions and have experts on staff to help you at all times.

Gardener's Supply also sells suet, which I use for my bird feeders, as well as really cool lawn ornaments and Christmas decorations. I bought pussy willow Christmas lights from them this year, and the first day that I lit them, my brand new kitten, Buttons, chewed through the wire, which meant the lights no longer worked. After I explained my situation, Gardener's Supply was kind enough to sell me another set at half-price. In the end, my electrician fixed the set that

Buttons chewed so I now have two sets, which worked out, because the kitten chewed through the wire, again (and, no, I am not getting rid of the cat).

RAISED BED HEIRLOOM ORGANIC GARDENS

What makes a plant or seed heirloom is that it originates from early periods in human history, it is not used in large-scale agriculture, and it has kept its original traits.

Growing up, my family lived in the country. We always had a big garden, as there were six people in our family, including four growing children. My Mom and Grandmom would always freeze and can everything that they could get their hands on and, as kids, we would help pull weeds, clean corn, harvest, or whatever else needed to be done. All winter long, we could then eat what had been harvested and stored. As an adult, I moved to town, and, for many years, I had my few tomato plants in pots, along with some herb plants. I guess you can take the girl out of the country, but you cannot take the country out of the girl.

My gardening bug kept getting itchier and itchier, and I prayed for God to send someone to help teach me how to correctly do heirloom organic gardening. Lo and behold, Mr. Joe Morra of Morra Contracting and Heritage Creek Farm (www.heritagecreekfarm.net) in Audubon, PA, came into my life as a potlucker. Joe is a contractor by day and an heirloom organic gardener by night, so I hired him to build my raised beds (please see my website, www. livingdynamically.com, for pictures of my garden). Not only did he build my raised beds for me, but he taught me so much about heirloom organic gardening, as well. I am sure he eventually got tired of me calling and saying, "Joe can I [fill in the blank]." Not to mention the running joke that I always want to grow plants that are indigenous to other parts of the world. For example, my brother lives in Florida, and had given me an orange tree for Christmas a few years ago, which I place outside in my own yard in Pennsylvania. Yes, it is still alive, and I have to bring it in every winter, but I do get baby oranges on it. I would also really love to grow avocados, but they do not grow in the colder climates of the Northeast, either.

The first year that I had the raised beds, we had a lot of rain in my area. Everyone's gardens were washed out except for mine (I just figured that God was taking care of the watering for me). My garden my first year divinely exceeded everyone else's, including all the local experts. This may, in part, be due to the fact that I used raised beds, which I have found to be much easier to maintain, as they require less weeding. You can also rotate your crops more easily with raised beds. Yet, for me, the greatest advantage is they are just plain pretty. One of the happiest places on earth is standing or sitting in the center of my garden. In the warmer months, you will always find me outside, enjoying the view of my garden. Besides having fresh vegetables just by walking out my back door every day, I have a constant reason to be outside in the fresh air, sun, and soil, which recharges me emotionally and spiritually.

I have eight raised beds that are each three feet by twelve feet by nine inches. My garden is fenced in to keep the animals out (they like heirloom organic vegetables, too). You can either have a local contractor build you a garden, like I did, or you can go to your local gardening supply store and purchase a precut raised bed kit. If you purchase a kit, all that you need to do is nail it together, fill it with soil, and put down the black cloth to keep the weeds down. I really like the black cloth, because I have noticed that it makes a huge difference with weeding and can be used year after year. I bought a big roll of it, and it is still up in my shed: I am still reusing the black cloth from my first year of gardening.

After you make your initial investment of setting up your garden, the ongoing yearly investment is minimal. All that you really need to do each year is buy seeds and add new fertilizer to pep up the soil.

I only have half of an acre, so my garden is living proof that you do not need a large farm of forty acres to have a prosperous harvest. I live in town, and have turned my yard into an oasis with everything from an apple tree to raspberry and blueberry plants that I eat fresh and freeze for the winter.

DEHYDRATED SOUP

One way to store your vegetables from your garden is to dehydrate them. I use Tribest's Sedona Dehydrator. Some day, I would like to have a solar dehydrator built, as referenced in Eben Fodor's book, *The Solar Food Dryer*. I like the idea of a solar dehydrator so I can tap into our natural resource: the sun. Plus, if the electricity goes out, I can still use a solar dehydrator. Dehydrated vegetables can be rehydrated with water to create a soup. Pull out your slow-cooker and set it at the lowest setting, so it is below 118°F. Throw the dried vegetables into the slow-cooker, along with fresh, sliced mushrooms and frozen corn, tomatoes, or any of your favorite frozen vegetables. Add a dash of salt and pepper to taste. When I freeze corn and tomatoes, I make sure to still keep it raw. My Mom and I would freeze our corn and tomatoes together, and she would always cook hers for the full length of time, as she was not into raw foods. I would instead only cook mine for a quarter or half of the required time, so it would still be considered "raw," but cooked enough to preserve. When I serve my soup, I also top it with croutons (remember to save your almond pulp when you make almond milk, so you can make your own croutons). The croutons, besides being great on soups and salads, make a great snack.

CREAMED CORN CASSEROLE

My family has a recipe for creamed corn casserole, which contains creamed corn, salt, pepper, egg, milk, sugar, and flour, which is baked in the oven. This is a to-die-for recipe, but since I no longer eat a standard American diet, I had to come up with a way to make it raw.

In a mixing bowl, combine creamed corn, salt and pepper to taste, and agave. Place in a glass bowl and dehydrate to complete the creamed corn casserole. I typically have to dehydrate it for eight to twelve hours in order to achieve the desired consistency. I sometimes make the creamed corn by adding almond milk. I have also added flax seeds and/or flax meal. Do not be afraid to make simple changes like this to switch it up and see what texture and taste you like best.

GARDENING IN URBAN AREAS AND SMALL SPACES

If you live in the city or in a condo, you can still maintain a successful garden. Besides sprouting (see below for basic sprouting directions and *Raw Inspiration* for further details), you can grow plants in Earth Boxes on your balconies or under grow lights inside your apartment all year round. If you have a condo or tiny backyard, Earth Boxes would work great for you, as well. I even line my driveway with Earth Boxes and plant my string beans and snow peas in them. You can purchase Earth Boxes online or from the Home Shopping Network.

For basic sprouting, all that you need is a glass jar, water, and seeds. Place a screen or material netting on top of a jar, and then secure the netting with a thick rubber band. Put one to two tablespoons of seeds in the jar and cover with water over night. The next morning, pour off the water, rinse the seeds, and lay the jar on its side. Rinse the seeds twice a day and harvest at the desired height.

I also have planter pots that I fill with all of my herbs. I love being able to walk out my kitchen door and clip my fresh herbs to use in whatever food that I am preparing. You can also dehydrate (dry) your fresh herbs and store them for use during the winter. I even grow catnip for my cats, and it is so funny to see them sleeping or sitting on top of the potted catnip plants. You can start herbs in the seed starting trays just as you would with vegetables. When you plant your herbs outside, you can either plant them in pots like I do or in the ground.

Dehydrating your herbs or vegetables for preserving is really quite simple. For vegetables like tomatoes, start cutting them into slices, place them on a dehydrator tray at 105°F, and dehydrate until dry. I also dehydrate my tomatoes with various seasonings and eat them as a snack or crumble them on top of a salad. When dehydrating herbs, you would use the same principle, making sure to first remove any stems. Herbs typically take very little time to dehydrate, so be sure to keep an eye on the dehydrator. Dehydration is a great way to preserve, and you can also rehydrate any dehydrated vegetables by simply adding water.

If you really want the results of gardening, but do not have much space, most areas have community gardens, urban gardens, and CSAs (Community Supported Agricultures) that you can participate in. Many towns also have farmers markets that carry organic vegetables. Some farmers markets, like mine in Phoenixville, PA, even run year-round, so you can enjoy fresh, organic foods even during the winter. In fact, trips to the farmers market can even be a great Saturday morning meeting place to socialize while you shop. I love the fact that farmers markets have brought back the sense of community that we all used to have, but somehow have lost with busy work schedules.

LISA'S FAVORITE BOOKS ON GARDENING

Rodale's All-New Encyclopedia of Organic Gardening, Fern Marshall Bradley and Barbara W. Ellis

Rodale's Illustrated Encyclopedia of Herbs, Claire Kowalchik and William H. Hylton

Burpee Complete Gardener: A Comprehensive, Up-to-Date, Fully Illustrated Reference for Gardeners at All Levels, Allan Armitage, Maureen Heffernan, Chela Kleiber, and Holly H. Shimizu

The Organic Gardener's Handbook of Natural Pest and Disease Control: A Complete Guide to Maintaining a Healthy Garden and Yard the Earth-Friendly Way, Fern Marshall Bradley, Barbara W. Ellis, and Deborah L. Martin

Home Composting Made Easy, C. Forrest McDowell, Ph. D., and Tricia Clark-McDowell

Four-Season Harvest: Organic Vegetables from Your Home Garden All Year Long, Eliot Coleman and Barbara Damrosch

The Gardener's A-Z Guide to Growing Organic Food, Tanya L. K. Denckla

Carrots Love Tomatoes: Secrets of Companion Planting for Successful Gardening, Louise Riotte

Grow Vegetables: Gardens, Yard, Balconies, Roof Terraces, Alan Buckingham and Jo Whittingham

The Veggie Gardener's Answer Book, Solutions to Every Problem You'll Ever Face, Answers to Every Question You'll Ever Ask, Barbara W. Ellis

Microgreens: A Guide to Growing Nutrient-Packed Greens, Eric Franks and Jasmine Richardson

The Heirloom Tomato: From Garden to Table: Recipes, Portraits and History of the World's Most Beautiful Fruit, Amy Goldman

Perelandra Garden Workbook II: Co-Creative Energy Processes for Gardening, Agriculture and Life, Machaelle Small Wright

The Findhorn Garden: Pioneering a New Vision of Man and Nature in Cooperation, The Findhorn Community

Flower Essence Repertory, A Comprehensive Guide to the Flower Essences Researched by Dr. Edward Bach and the Flower Essence Society, Patricia Kaminski and Richard Katz

Seed to Seed: Seed Saving and Growing Techniques for Vegetable Gardeners, Suzanne Ashworth

How to Store Your Garden Produce: The Key to Self-Sufficiency, Piers Warren

Micro Eco-Farming: Prospering from Backyard to Small Acreage in Partnership with the Earth, Barbara Berst Adams

Organic Seed Production and Saving: The Wisdom of Plant Heritage, Brian Connolly

The Resilient Gardener: Food Production and Self-Reliance in Uncertain Times, Carol Deppe

Roses Love Garlic: Companion Planting and Other Secrets of Flowers, Louise Riotte

The Truth About Gardening Remedies: What Works, What Doesn't, and Why, Jeff Gillman

The Vegetable Gardener's Bible, Edward C. Smith

Wicked Plants: The A-Z of Plants that Kill, Maim, Intoxicate and Otherwise Offend, Amy Stewart

Here are my bee hives. I had my hives painted light green instead of the traditional white to blend in with nature.

MASTERING THE ART OF BEEKEEPING

When I transitioned to a healthy diet sixteen years ago, I never would have dreamed that I would end up becoming a beekeeper. It was something that I had wanted to do for several years. Some people tried to talk me out of it and others started beekeeping when I did and totally got it. I cannot exactly explain why I was so drawn to bees before I got into them; it was just another one of those divinely-led situations that continuously happens . . . I am so thankful that God is in my life.

> The man who follows the crowd will usually get no further than the crowd. The man who walks alone is likely to find himself in places no one has ever been before.
>
> —ANONYMOUS

If you are interested in beekeeping, the first step would be to check your local ordinances to see if you can keep bees in your area, and to find out about any regulations on how far your hives must be set back from your property lines. No matter where you place your hive, you will find that your eyes are drawn to that location any time that you are out and about in your yard.

Once you have some information on local requirements, you will want to learn all the basics before getting started. I went to Bee School to learn the "Art of Beekeeping" from Jim Bob and Scott Bartow of Liberty Bee Honey Farms in Worcester, PA. Jim and Scott are two walking encyclopedias of bee knowledge, and they patiently and graciously shared their knowledge with me no matter how many times I asked the same question. I am always so grateful when someone is willing to share their knowledge. Jim began his "bee" career as "Mr. Bee" of the county, until word of his vast knowledge spread throughout the state; and now, his jurisdiction ranges from Canada to South America (east of Mississippi).

Scott's degree is in Environmental Forest Biology, and he spent the first ten years of his career working with primates at the Philadelphia Zoo in Philadelphia, PA. He then worked on Wall Street, but decided to make a change when the market crashed. At the time, his wife (then fiancé) was living near Philadelphia, PA, and Scott decided to move there so he could pursue his dream of beekeeping, and he now works with Jim. In fact, they increased their hives last year by adding 100 additional hives located at Longwood Gardens in Chaddsford, PA. If you are ever in the area, be sure to make a trip to Longwood Gardens. The property was once a Dupont estate, and is world renowned for its gardens. I have been a friend of Longwood Gardens for several years, and have been going there for as long as I can remember. Besides learning a lot about all types of gardening from their year-round activities and classes, it is just a beautiful place to escape from the world. They also have restaurants in case you get hungry while you enjoy the gardens.

Jim and Scott do hold classes every year, and will teach you everything that you need to know to set up your hives and bees. You can also purchase basic beekeeping supplies from them, if necessary. Jim and Scott start by teaching you about the basic equipment that you will need to get started. They also teach you the anatomy and habits of the honey bee. As the season progresses, they teach you how to feed and care for your bees, how to harvest the honey in the fall, and how to winterize your bees in the cold months.

For my first year, I started with three hives, which allowed me to compare the activities of each hive. This was a great learning tool, because it showed me what made each hive strong or weak. At the end of the season, the three hives remained as they had started out: one was the strongest, another was average, and the weakest hive did not make it (the queen died and was not replaced). Perhaps if I had been aware when the queen had died in the weakest hive, I could have done more, but this happened right after my Mom died, so I was not as attentive as I might normally be. Although there is a lot to learn, the good news is the bees are smart and do most of the work themselves.

When you start beekeeping, you may find that some of your neighbors are resistant to the idea. For example, my neighbor to the back of my property was upset when he saw that I was going to have bees. He was worried that my bees would infest his house and attack his children. I explained to him that my honey bees would not infest his house, as they had their own houses. In addition, honey bees do not attack people and/or animals unless their house is disturbed in some way. I informed him that the only way my bees would attack his children would be if they climbed the fence onto my property and started opening the hives. So, if you are looking to keep bees, but are concerned about your kids, do not bee (that was a bee pun). In fact, my dogs often walk up and put their noses at the lower opening of the hives where the bees enter and exit, and they have never been stung. If you have an upset neighbor like I did, calmly explain to them that they are not in any danger, and that the bees are harmless unless provoked. On the other hand, you may find that some neighbors are excited that you are getting bees, because it will help their plants grow better.

I love the fact that my back lawn looks like an international airport when the trees are in bloom and the bees are out gathering pollen. They fly out of their hives, go straight up over the blueberry plants, and take off. When studying bees and beekeeping, the knowledge that you obtain is truly fascinating. For example, you may not have known that bees can travel up to one-and-a-half miles away from their hive, and that the size of the comb should be three-eighths of an inch: no more, no less. Honey was also used as part of burial traditions in ancient Egypt. Because honey will keep forever, the pharaohs would store honey in the pyramids so that they would have something to eat when they came back to life. You also may already know that honey is great for cooking, candle-making, and soap-making, but did you know that it is also extremely medicinal because of its antibacterial and antifungal properties? There are so many more interesting facts that you can learn about bees and honey once you start researching.

LISA'S FAVORITE BOOKS ON BEEKEEPING

Beekeeping Basics (Formerly Fundamentals of Beekeeping), Maryann Frazier

The Beekeeper's Handbook, Diana Sammataro, Alphonse Avitabile, and Roger A. Morse

The Hive and the Honey Bee, published by Dadant & Sons

The ABC and XYZ of Bee Culture, A. I. Root and E. R. Root

Honey: The Gourmet Medicine, Joe Traynor

Keeping Bees and Making Honey, Alison Benjamin and Brian McCallum

Beeswax Crafts: Candlemaking, Modelling, Beauty Creams, Soaps and Polishes, Encaustic Art, Wax Crayons, Norman Battershill

American Bee Journal (periodical)

Bee Culture (periodical)

No matter where you live, you can go online and look up your local bee-keeper's association, which can be a great resource for information and learning opportunities. I am a member of my county and state's beekeepers associations. My county association holds monthly meetings where local beekeepers get together and learn from guest speakers. I also plan on taking classes again next year at Liberty Bee Honey Farm to help me learn how to better care for my bees and to learn more about bees in general.

You will find that beekeeping, while a great experience, does require a bit of patience. I did not get any honey for my own use during the first year, because all the honey from the first year is for the bees. The second year, I will be able to harvest honey for myself; I can hardly wait.

Living the raw lifestyle and doing things like beekeeping may seem like it would be expensive. Yet I am thrifty, I live this lifestyle, and it works for me. Even my bees are thrifty. For example, when you work your bees, you use a smoker to send smoke into the hive, which brings the bees back into the hive. The fuel for the smoker is simply old leaves, pine needles, or left-over paper towel and toilet paper rolls. There are lots of ways that you can reuse other materials to save money and make beekeeping affordable.

KEEPING CHICKENS

You may be wondering why a vegetarian would have eight chickens. Well, it all started when I was a child, and my family had a little Banty hen named Gertrude. Gertrude was so sweet, and she quickly became a member of our family. Once in awhile, she would lay a little egg. As you can tell, we did not keep her because of her egg-laying capacity, but because we loved her. Our chicken journey continued when my brother, Dennis, was in high school, and

Here are my Girls—Tiger and Freckles

he got a leghorn rooster named Rolf. Rolf was just the opposite of Gertrude. As sweet and loving as Gertrude was, Rolf was equally mean and nasty. When I was a little girl, he would chase me across the lawn and attack me. When Rolf was out, the only place that I was ever safe on the back lawn was on top of the picnic table. I must confess that I was not sorry to see him pass years later. The funny thing about Rolf was he would make this funny chicken noise whenever he heard someone sneeze. This was especially amusing if we had company over and someone sneezed. The guests would look at each other and wonder what the noise was.

The wonderful benefit with chickens is not only that they give you the gift of eggs to nourish your body, but they also make great pets. Sitting out in the chicken yard is one of the best stress relievers. You can have chickens, put food on your table, and have them also be your buddies.

Years later, I was visiting a friend in California, and noticed that they had free-range heritage chickens and turkeys. It was such a treat for me to feed the chickens, because it brought back fond childhood memories. I loved it when we were preparing food in the kitchen, and the birds would come to the front windows to watch us. Plus, whenever I walked outside, they would follow me; I loved every minute of it. I promised myself that, someday, I would get chickens. I assumed that day would come if I ever moved to the country.

That day, however, came sooner than I had originally expected. I am a planner and an organizer, so the first thing that I did when I got home from California was to visit my borough hall and ask if I would be able to keep chickens in town. I was told that I could, as long as my neighbors did not mind. So, I stuck this knowledge in the back of my mind and did not think about it much until March, 2010, when I walked into my local feed store. The first thing that I noticed was they had a large assortment of chicks (which I call "peepies"), and they even had chicken house kits on sale (two of my favorite words after "free" are "on sale"). So, I ended up buying eight peepies, four Rhode Island Reds, and four Americanas. I bought Rhode Island Reds because they are good for laying eggs and are a heritage breed (heritage to chickens is like heirloom to seeds). I also like that the Rhode Island Reds lay beige eggs. I bought the Americanas because I was told that they would lay turquoise eggs. They do not lay nearly as many eggs as the Rhode Island Reds, but the Americanas are even more personable than the Rhode Island Reds. A friend of mine even keeps a rooster as a pet. It lives in the bushes outside their back door in the summer time, and, in the winter, they put him in a dog crate covered by a tarp. My brother used to keep his rooster in our basement in a box with a screen on top. I also have three miniature chickens, and, in the winter, I keep them in little peepie cages on my dining room table.

Once I got my peepies home, I kept them in their cage on my dining room table with a heat lamp on. I eventually moved them to my garage, and, once it was warm enough outside, and they grew bigger and had their feathers, I released them to their chicken yard. A friend and his family assembled my chicken house and built a fenced yard for my chickens. The fencing covered the top and sides to prevent the chickens from flying out of the yard. The fence also helps to protect my chickens by keeping out wildlife. I never realized that my sweet little chickens could have so many enemies: I had friends who sadly lost some of their chickens to foxes, raccoons, and hawks. Because of my fencing (thank God), I did not lose any of my chickens.

I should note that I only bought girls (hens) when I got chickens, because I live in town and did not want any of my neighbors to complain about a rooster crowing at four or five o'clock in the morning. My neighbors on the corner do know that I have chickens, and I even invited them over to meet "the girls," because they love animals as much as I do. They fell in love with them: so much so that when their daughters came to town, they asked if they could introduce them to the chickens. I always giggle when people come over to my house, because they generally either want to go see my garden or my chickens.

So, why have chickens if you are a vegetarian? I asked myself that same question. Even when following a raw diet, you can still enjoy the benefits of eating eggs. Twice a week, I put one raw egg in my daily breakfast smoothie. Eggs are full of B12, which is necessary for normal red blood cell formation, as well as tissue and cellular repair. If you do not have enough B12, you can develop anemia, a condition in which the blood does not have enough healthy red blood cells to provide oxygen to the body tissue. I can also barter with my eggs or give them as gifts to those who have blessed my heart. I also save the feathers, which ended up being used by my friend's little boy, who makes dream catchers.

Chickens are also great foragers and control all manner of pests like ticks, grasshoppers, and mosquitoes. They also are great fertilizers. I use their excretions and place it on my garden. Every book that I read says how great chicken excretions are for fertilizing your garden.

In the raw lifestyle, you will find that you can reuse everything. For example, once I am finished removing the meat and liquid of my young Thai coconuts, I give the shell to my parrot as a toy to help him sharpen his beak. It turns out that the chickens like coconut shells, as well. In fact, they adore all of my table scraps (except banana skins). When I juice a watermelon, I give the chickens the rind, and, after a few hours, it is already cleaned down to the skin. When I go out to dinner with friends and they do not take their leftovers, I ask if I can have them for my chickens. My chickens also really love pumpkins. Before giving the pumpkin to your chickens, you can cut out the meat and turn it into a pâté, and then mix the seeds in seasonings and dehydrate them. As you can see, my chickens eat very well. I do not even need to compost any more now that I have chickens.

Once you eat eggs from your own chickens, you will notice a vast difference in taste. Every single person to whom I have given eggs has said the difference in taste is night and day between my chickens' eggs and store-bought eggs. This is because eggs bought in stores are dipped in formaldehyde, which is a carcinogen. Plus, my eggs are fresh, and there is no telling how old eggs are when purchased from your local market.

HOW TO WINTERIZE YOUR CHICKENS

If you are a concerned "Mom" to your chickens (like I am), you will want to make sure that they are comfortable during the cold winter months. Here are some things that you can do to winterize your chickens:

> Put plastic sheeting on the chickens' fencing and roof to keep out the rain, wind, and snow. Do not place sheeting on the door in the chicken yard, as you want to allow fresh air to come in.

> When applying plastic sheeting, you can also put wooden lathe on the roof of the fence to offset the weight of potential heavy rains and snow.

> Add a solar light to turn on in the winter to help compensate for the dwindling day light. Use a heating tray for their water dish to keep their water from freezing.

Another great reason to keep chickens is that they are a lot of fun. Certain breeds, such as Rhode Island Reds and Americanas, are known to be particularly sociable, but you will notice that each of your chickens can have their own personalities, as well. It is such a delight to go out to my chicken yard every day to feed them, and sit with them while they roam about and play. It is one of the happiest, most peaceful parts of my day. In the time that I have had my chickens, I have bonded with them and have even named each one: there are Freckles, Golden Girl, Cleopatra, Tiger, Big Red, Little Red, Pinky, and Lee. They all let me pet them, and I can even pick them up. I am not the only one who shares such an enthusiasm for my chickens. When I get together with friends who also have chickens, we start talking about our chickens, and swap chicken stories and pictures like folks do about their grandkids. Other people look at us like we are nuts, but I just love my girls, and I would not trade them for anything in the world.

LISA'S FAVORITE BOOKS ON KEEPING CHICKENS

Chickens: Celebrating America's Favorite Farm Animals (periodical)

Mother Earth News (periodical)

Keeping Chickens! Tending Small Flocks in Cities, Suburbs, and Other Small Spaces, Barbara Kilarski

Storey's Guide to Raising Poultry: Breeds, Care, Health, Leonard Mercia

Storey's Guide to Raising Chickens: Care, Feeding, Facilities, Gail Damerow

WHO ME, A FARMER?

It is funny: I never considered myself a farmer until, one day, my neighbor called me a farmer; my neighbor explained, "Well, you have a garden, berry plants, chickens, and bees. You're a farmer." I had not thought about it that way. I just assumed that, because I did not live on forty acres, I could not possibly be considered a farmer. Yet the truth is, whether we live on 40 acres, half of an acre, or simply plant a few herbs on a balcony, when we create some of our own food supply, I guess that makes us farmers.

For years now, I have been reading about global food shortages and the possibility of severe shortages in the future. So, not only does it make sense to grow your own food for health and economical reasons, but also to ensure the availability of food for you and your loved ones. Participating in growing some of your own food is another way of taking back control of your life, your health, and your well-being. If you want to live dynamically, you need to step up to the plate (or pick up the hoe, in this case), and start planning your garden today.

I realize that some of you may never plant a garden or an Earth Box, but you can still gain control over what you eat by becoming a contributing member of a CSA. By pulling your resources together, you can buy in bulk, buy direct, and eliminate the middle man (grocery stores). You can also start shopping at farmers markets in your town. Think about how you can help yourself, your family, and your community. It may only start with one tomato plant today, but, tomorrow, it could be a whole orchard.

Asparagus Salad

Joel Odhner, Catalyst Cleanse, Rawlife Line, Philadelphia, PA

Prep: 20 minutes

1 pound asparagus, chopped
1 red pepper, diced
1 yellow pepper, diced
½ cup parsley, chopped
3 scallions, chopped
Zest of 1 orange
1 orange, juiced
1 lemon, juiced
2 tablespoons cold-pressed olive oil
Sea salt to taste

Toss all ingredients together and let stand for 1 hour. Lasts 2–3 days when refrigerated.

Basic Kale Salad

Lisa Montgomery

Everyone seems to have a basic kale salad in their salad repertoire. The good news about kale is that it is full of vitamins, minerals, and even protein. One of the most commonly asked questions of a raw foodist is where you should get your protein. My answer always is, "From everything I eat." Kale has more protein than meat, and it is easily assimilated. Kale goes through my system far better than meat ever went through my body; I just did not know it until transitioning to a raw diet.

Prep: 20 minutes

1–2 bunches kale, stems removed and chopped into bite-sized
      pieces
1 cup tomato (fresh or sun-dried), diced
1–2 avocados, chopped
1 red pepper, chopped
1–2 tablespoons hemp seeds, hulled
2½ tablespoons pumpkin seed oil (try Austria's Finest)
1½ tablespoons lemon juice
1 teaspoon Celtic sea salt

Combine all of the ingredients together in a mixing bowl, using your hands to make sure that they are well blended, and that the kale is well-coated. Serve immediately.

This keeps extremely well when refrigerated.

Rainbow Salad

Elaina Love, Elaina's Pure Joy Kitchen: Raw, Organic, Vegan Recipes
(www.PureJoyPlanet.com)

*Elaina said this is one of her most popular salads. I've made this recipe
and loved it. Not only does it taste great but I love all the colors and
textures.*

Prep: 30 minutes
Serves: 8

Almond Mayonnaise
1 cup soaked almonds (½ cup before soaking)
¾ cup water
1 clove garlic
½ teaspoon Celtic sea salt or 1 tablespoon tamari
3 tablespoons lemon juice or 1½ tablespoons apple cider vinegar
½ teaspoon Italian seasoning
3 large dates or 3 tablespoons honey or maple syrup
Dash of cayenne pepper
1½–2 cups flax or olive oil

Salad
½ red cabbage, shredded
2 large carrots, shredded
3 broccoli stalks and 1½ heads, shredded
4 scallions, thinly sliced
1 cup raisins
¼ cup sliced almonds
1½ cups almond mayonnaise
½ teaspoon mustard powder
½ teaspoon ginger powder
½ teaspoon garlic powder
1–2 teaspoons Celtic sea salt or 4–6 tablespoons tamari

Almond Mayonnaise

Peel almonds for a whiter mayonnaise. Place all ingredients (except the oil) in a blender. Blend until creamy. Put your blender on a low speed, and drizzle the oil through the hole in the blender lid. Add oil until the mixture becomes thick.

Salad

Combine above ingredients with half the almond mayonnaise recipe.

Zen Cabbage Salad

Joel Odhner, Catalyst Cleanse, Rawlife Line, Philadelphia, PA

Prep: 20–30 minutes
Marinate: 10 minutes

2 cups green cabbage
1 teaspoon sea salt
2 tablespoons sesame oil (or toasted sesame oil)
1 teaspoon lemon juice
¼ cup sesame seeds (or hemp or chia seeds)

Combine cabbage and salt in a bowl, massaging the salt into the cabbage. Let sit for 10 minutes. Add the remaining ingredients (except the sesame seeds) and mix well. Alternatively, you can also combine all the ingredients in a bowl and massage all together. Add sesame seeds before serving.

You can also add purple cabbage, slivers of carrots, and red peppers. I love adding these because, besides tasting great, they also make the dish look beautiful. Plus, when your garden is cranking, you have it all at your fingertips to use, so you may as well use it.

Hemp Cabbage Salad

Joel Odhner, Catalyst Cleanse, Rawlife Line, Philadelphia, PA

Prep: 20–30 minutes
Marinate: 10 minutes

½ head red and green cabbage, shredded
¼ cup lemon juice
¼ cup cold-pressed olive oil
¼ cup favorite seasoning mix
Pinch sea salt
¼ cup hemp seeds

Shred cabbage in a food processor. Combine cabbage with the remaining ingredients in a mixing bowl, making sure that it is well-blended, and that the cabbage leaves are coated. Let stand for 10 minutes.

Napa Cabbage Cole Slaw

Tonya Zavasta, Beautiful on Raw: Uncooked Creations

I have had the pleasure of having Tonya speak at my raw potlucks and, in addition to being a gifted speaker and having a dear heart, she is one of the most beautiful women I have ever met. She has the most amazing skin.

Prep: 20 minutes

1 cup shredded Napa cabbage
¼ medium red onion, diced
½ green bell pepper, chopped
½ cup shredded Granny Smith apples
¼ cup chopped fresh dill
2 tablespoons olive oil
Juice of medium lemon
Sea salt to taste

In a large salad bowl, combine all ingredients. Toss until well coated. Allow to stand 15 minutes and serve. Will keep refrigerated for 1–2 days.

Alorah's Asian Broccoli Salad

Alorah Arliotis (www.thewiserwoman.co.uk), Glastonbury, England

Prep: 20 minutes

1 head broccoli
1 red pepper, thinly sliced
Small piece fresh ginger, finely chopped
1 clove garlic, crushed or finely chopped
Nama shoyu
Olive oil (for soaking)
Sea vegetables
Fresh coriander or cilantro, chopped, to garnish

Cut and marinate the broccoli in red pepper, ginger, garlic, nama shoyu and olive oil. Sprinkle sea vegetables with finely chopped fresh cilantro on top.

Avocado Salad with Ginger Dressing

Lisa Montgomery

Prep: 35 minutes

Avocado Salad

1 avocado, diced

1–2 bags spring mixed greens (or cut fresh from your own garden)

1 large apple, diced and/or sliced into bite-sized pieces

1 teaspoon sesame seeds

¼ cup dried cranberries (whole or finely chopped into bite-sized pieces)

Ginger Dressing

1 clove garlic

Small piece ginger (about the size of your pinky), grated

¾ cup olive oil

½ cup apple cider vinegar

1 tablespoon agave or raw honey

Avocado Salad

Combine the ingredients in bowl and toss.

Ginger Dressing

Combine all the ingredients in a blender on high speed. Adjust to taste (for example, if you want the dressing more tart, add more apple cider vinegar; if you would like your dressing sweet, add agave or raw honey).

When entertaining, I prefer to serve this dressing on the side and let my guests add as little or as much dressing as they like on the avocado salad.

Ginger Salad Dressing

Laura Sipes Wright (YouTube: StarFlower99654)

You can also use this dressing on the Avocado Salad on page 41.

Prep: 30 minutes
Soak: while you are working prepping second set of ingredients
(about 30 minutes)

First Set of Ingredients:
¼ cup raw ketchup
2 tablespoons fresh tomato, diced
1 date, pitted and diced
2 tablespoons sun-dried tomato
¼ cup soaking water

Second Set of Ingredients:
¼ cup ginger root, grated
¼ cup celery, minced
1 cup onion, minced
1 clove garlic, minced
1 teaspoon sea salt
½ teaspoon ground black pepper
1 cup cold-pressed olive oil
⅔ cup apple cider vinegar
2 tablespoons + 2 teaspoons nama shoyu or wheat-free tamari
2 tablespoons + 2 teaspoons raw honey
2 tablespoons + 2 teaspoons lemon juice

First Set of Ingredients:
Soak all ingredients for 30 minutes. Once ketchup soaking ingredients have finished soaking, blend together in a high-speed blender and set aside.

Second Set of Ingredients:
Combine all ingredients with the soaked ingredients and blend on high speed. Add the soaking water, if necessary, to reach the desired thickness.

Watercress Salad

Joel Odhner, Catalyst Cleanse, Rawlife Line, Philadelphia, PA

Prep: 15–20 minutes

2 bunches watercress
1 large Asian pear
¼ cup cold-pressed extra virgin olive oil
¼ cup maple syrup (optional)
Lemon pepper to taste

Toss all the ingredients and serve.

Watercress, like mustard greens, is a cruciferous vegetable and, like its cousins broccoli and cabbage, has been recognized as an important source of calcium, iron, and folic acid. It is one of the oldest known leafy greens eaten by humans. Perhaps the best incentive to add this delicious green to your culinary repertoire is the exciting research that came out of the University of Ulster (United Kingdom) about the anti-cancer properties of watercress. This study found that daily intake of watercress can significantly reduce an important cancer trigger; namely DNA damage to white blood cells. Eating watercress salad has also been shown to lower cholesterol and improve absorption of lutein and beta carotene, which are key minerals for eye health and the prevention of age-related conditions such as cataracts.

When eaten raw, watercress is prized for its peppery flavor. You can also mix watercress with fruit for a variety of flavor sensations.

If you are lucky enough to live near Alresford, Hampshire, in the United Kingdom, you can attend their annual Watercress Festival in the spring. There is also a newer watercress festival in Osceola, Wisconsin.

As a child, my neighbors grew watercress in their creek. Now that I know all of the amazing health benefits of this vegetable, I am planning on growing it in a tub in my backyard, since I do not have a stream running through my yard. There are several websites that provide detailed instructions on how to grow watercress in containers on your back lawn, your balcony, and/or patio.

Chopped Beauty Salad

Janice Innella, The Beauty Chef

Of all the salads that I have had, Janice's is one of the best salads in regard to taste, eye appeal, and health benefits.

Prep: 30 minutes

½ head red cabbage, chopped

1 cup organic frozen corn (or fresh off the cob)

2 gala apples, chopped

4 leaves kale, stems removed

1 cup dried cranberries or pomegranates

1 cup fresh basil

½ cup pumpkin seeds (try Austria's Finest, Naturally), ground
      (or golden flax)

Juice of 2 lemons (or juice of Valencia oranges)

1 teaspoon sea salt

3 tablespoons pumpkin seed oil (try Austria's Finest, Naturally)

2 red peppers, chopped

1 avocado, diced

1 blood orange (for garnish)

Process all the ingredients (except the peppers and avocado) in a food processor. Once processed, stir in the peppers and avocado. Combine all together and serve, garnished with the blood orange.

Beggin' for Bangkok Broccoli Bombast Bonanza

Potlucker Mary Kane

Prep: 30–45 minutes

Salad

1 cup broccoli, diced

½ cup bok choy, diced

½ cup Fuji apple, diced

1 cup zucchini, finely sliced on angle

½ cup fresh turmeric, diced (optional)

1 cup celery, finely chopped

2 cloves garlic, finely sliced

4 tablespoons ginger, diced

1 Thai coconut (meat only), chopped

½ cup red bell pepper, cut thin

1 yellow squash, cut into spirals

½ cup fresh herbs (parsley, cilantro, and rosemary), diced

Dressing

½ cup citrus juice (blend ¾ orange and ¼ lime or lemon juice)

⅓ cup Moroccan olive water (or 2 teaspoons salt)

1 whole hot pepper of your choice

½ cup stone-crushed olive oil

Salad

Combine broccoli, bok choy, apple, zucchini, turmeric, celery, 1 clove of garlic, 1 tablespoon of ginger, coconut, bell pepper, squash, and fresh herbs in a large mixing bowl.

Dressing

In a high-speed blender, combine citrus-juice blend and olive water with the hot pepper and remaining garlic, turmeric, and ginger from the salad. Blend and add the olive oil.

You can cover the salad with the dressing or serve the dressing on the side. This dish will keep for up to 5 days in the refrigerator.

Fiesta Salad

Frederic Patenaude's New Year's Day Menu (www.fredericpatenaude. com)

Prep: 30 minutes

Salad
8 cups romaine lettuce, cut into bite-sized pieces
1 red bell pepper, washed, seeded, and chopped
1 tomato, cut into eighths
1 cup fresh corn
1 cup cucumber, sliced and cut into quarters
2 radishes, sliced and cut in quarters
½ cup jicama, julienne cut
½ cup chayote squash, julienne cut
¼ cup fresh cilantro leaves, stems removed and finely chopped

Dressing
½ cup cold-pressed extra virgin olive oil
½ cup fresh lemon or lime juice (or combination)
½ teaspoon Mexican chili powder seasoning
¼ teaspoon Celtic sea salt
¼ cup cilantro leaves

Salad
Mix all the ingredients together in a bowl, and then garnish with cilantro. Serve with Fiesta Dressing.

Dressing
Blend all the ingredients (except the cilantro) in a high-speed blender until smooth and creamy. Add cilantro and pulse chop for a few seconds.

Date Dill Slaw

Brenda Cobb, Founder of Living Foods Institute® and author of The Living Foods Lifestyle *(www.livingfoodsinstitute.com), (800) 844-9876*

Prep: 30 minutes

2 cups purple or green cabbage, chopped
½ cup carrots, chopped
½ cup yellow, orange or red pepper, chopped
½ cup green onions with tops, chopped
½ cup olive oil
½ cup lemon juice
2 teaspoons Celtic or Himalayan sea salt
2 tablespoons dried dill or 6 tablespoons fresh dill
6 medjool dates, pitted

Using a food processor, chop the cabbage into chunky pieces and put in a bowl. Do the same for the carrots and put in the bowl. Chop the pepper and green onions by hand and put in the bowl. Put the olive oil, lemon juice, sea salt, dill, and dates into another bowl. Mash up the dates so the dressing becomes creamy, but leave some of the dates in small chunks. Add the vegetables and toss.

Harvest Salad

Lisa Montgomery

Prep: 30 minutes
Dehydrate: 2–4 hours (optional)

1 head red cabbage, shredded or chopped (using a food
    processor or by hand)
5–6 carrots, shredded
1 cup raisins
1–2 tablespoons agave
1 tablespoon cinnamon (or more to taste)
½ red onion, finely diced
2–3 pears, finely chopped
Sea salt to taste
Ground black pepper to taste (I keep in my pepper grinder a
    combination of black, red, green, and white peppers)

Combine all of the ingredients together and pour into a glass
serving dish. Optional: you can place the glass serving dish in a
dehydrator until warmed (2–4 hours).

Zulu Red Cabbage Salad

Jan McGlashan, Winston Park, KwaZulu-Natal, South Africa

Prep: 25 minutes

Dressing
1 tablespoon agave
½ cup cold-pressed olive oil
2–3 tablespoons apple cider vinegar (reduce if too tart for your
        taste)
Water (add as needed)

Salad
1 head red cabbage, shredded
2–3 carrots, grated
4–5 spring onions or shallots, sliced
½ cup plump raisins
1 cup raw pecans
Sea salt and pepper to taste

Dressing
Blend all dressing ingredients in a high-speed blender. Adjust to
taste.

Salad
In a mixing bowl, combine all ingredients (except pecans). Add
dressing and mix well. Sprinkle with pecans on top.

Colorful Corn Salad

Roger Haeska and Karymyn Malone
(www.Howtogoraw.com, www.LightningSpeedFitness.com, and www.
KarmynMalone.com)

Prep: 20 minutes
Serves: 2

4 ears sweet corn, cut off cob
1 cup premium tomato, diced
½ cup diced orange bell pepper
½ cup fresh cilantro, chopped
1 scallion, finely chopped
1 tomatillo, diced
1 tablespoon jalapeño pepper, minced
Juice of one lemon or lime

Mix all ingredients in a large bowl and enjoy.

Celery Root Slaw

Janice Innella, The Beauty Chef

Prep: 30 minutes

2 celery roots
4 gala apples
1 teaspoon cinnamon
1 red beet
½-1 cup dried cranberries
1 bunch basil
1 bunch Italian parsley
½ teaspoon Celtic sea salt
1 teaspoon orange zest or 1 whole orange
2 limes, juiced

Combine all the ingredients in your food processor and pulse chop, adding lemon juice and orange zest last. Serve with butter lettuce.

Beauty Butter Cups with Lemon Vinaigrette

Janice Innella, The Beauty Chef

Prep: 45 minutes

Salad

1 head butter lettuce
1 head bok choy, finely chopped
1 avocado, cubed
1 tablespoon dulse, ground

Dressing

1 cup lemon juice
½ cup pine nuts
½ cup cold-pressed olive oil
1 tablespoon umeboshi plum paste
1 tablespoon mustard powder
1 clove garlic

Salad

Clean all the greens. Carefully take apart the butter lettuce and pile into cups, making 2 large or 4 small. Place the bok choy inside the cups, and then add the cubed avocado. Sprinkle ground dulse on top.

Dressing

Combine all the ingredients in a high-speed blender. You can choose to either pour the dressing on top of the butter cups or serve on the side for your guests to serve themselves.

Broccoli Miso Salad

Brenda Cobb, Founder of Living Foods Institute® and author of The Living Foods Lifestyle *(www.livingfoodsinstitute.com), (800) 844-9876*

Prep: 20 minutes

3 cups broccoli
1 cup carrots
2 cloves garlic
3 tablespoons raw tahini
3 tablespoons chickpea miso
3 tablespoons lemon juice
2 tablespoons water

First peel the broccoli stems to leave a thin outer skin and then chop the broccoli stems and florets into small pieces in a food processor. Don't chop the broccoli so much that it becomes mushy. Leave it in small bite-sized pieces. Remove from the food processor and put into a bowl.

Next chop the carrots in the food processor. Take out and put in the bowl with the broccoli. Don't chop the broccoli and carrots together at the same time as the broccoli will become mushy before the carrots are chopped fine enough.

Next put the garlic in the food processor and chop, then add the raw tahini, chickpea miso, lemon juice, and water into the food processor and blend all together. You do not have to clean out the food processor of the broccoli and carrots before you make the dressing. Just put it all in and whatever residue of broccoli and carrots are left in the processor will be blended up in the dressing.

Take the dressing out of the food processor and mix with the broccoli and carrots. Toss well until all is coated.

Serve on a bed of mixed baby greens and enjoy!

Curry Cabbage Lentil Salad

Brenda Cobb, Founder of Living Foods Institute® and author of The Living Foods Lifestyle *(www.livingfoodsinstitute.com), (800) 844-9876*

Prep: 25 minutes

4 cups purple or green cabbage, chopped
3 large cloves garlic
1 cup green onion
1 cup red bell pepper
1 cup sprouted lentils
1 heaping tablespoon curry powder
½ cup lemon juice
½ cup olive oil
1 teaspoon Himalayan salt

Chop the cabbage in the food processor and set aside. Chop the garlic, onions, and red pepper by hand so they won't get mushy. Combine with the cabbage and lentils in a large bowl. Add the curry powder, lemon juice, olive oil, and sea salt to the vegetables and toss.

Corn Salad

Austria's Finest, Naturally, Helco Ltd., Mt. Vernon, VA
(www.austrianpumpkinoil.com)

I love Austria's Finest pumpkin seed oil and pumpkin seeds. They're both my all-time favorites.

Prep: 20 minutes
Serves: 2–3

16 ounces corn, cut off cob
Fresh garlic to taste (2 cloves recommended), minced
¼ medium bell pepper, diced
1 small Roma tomato, diced
2 tablespoons (or to taste) Austria's Finest, Naturally pumpkin
    seed oil
2 tablespoons (or to taste) raw apple cider vinegar (can
    substitute raw honey)
Salt and pepper to taste

Combine all ingredients together, mix well, and let stand at room temperature for at least one hour, mixing occasionally.

Tomato & Avocado Salad

Potlucker Peggy O'Neill

Prep: 20 minutes

8 plum tomatoes, sliced
2 avocados, chopped
Red onion, slivered, to taste
Jalapeño, sliced, to taste
Apple cider vinegar or balsamic vinegar to taste
Cold-pressed extra virgin olive oil to taste
Salt and pepper to taste

Combine all the ingredients, toss, and enjoy.

I prefer to use balsamic vinegar in place of apple cider vinegar, because I feel that the taste is far superior.

Austria's Finest, Naturally
Fall Harvest Salad

Austria's Finest, Naturally, Helco Ltd., Mt. Vernon, VA
(www.austrianpumpkinoil.com)

Serves 2–4
Prep: 30 minutes

1 apple, diced
1 pear, diced
1 bunch grapes (red or white), halved or quartered if using large
     grapes
1–2 ounces Austria's Finest, Naturally lightly salted pumpkin
     seeds
2 cups mixed garden salad greens or favorite lettuce
2 tablespoons Austria's Finest, Naturally pumpkin seed oil
1–2 tablespoons Austria's Finest, Naturally vinegar (depending
     on taste)

Dice the apple and pear, and then toss with the grapes, seeds, and
lettuce. Place individual servings on plates. Mix the oil and vinegar
(you can also add a dash of salt and pepper, if desired), and pour
over the salads. During the spring and summer, this makes a great
dressing.

Spring Goddess Salad

Janice Innella, the Beauty Chef

Prep: 30 minutes

1 head red Swiss chard
4 heads baby bok choy
1 bulb fennel
1 bunch asparagus, chopped
1 cup cashews, chopped
1 cup pumpkin seeds, ground (try Austria's Finest, Naturally)
½ bunch fresh dill, chopped
1 avocado, chopped
1½ cups fresh strawberries, sliced in half, plus more for garnish

Process the Swiss chard, bok choy, and fennel in a food processor and pour into a serving bowl. Mix with the asparagus, cashews, pumpkin seeds, dill, avocado, and strawberries. You can garnish the salad with more sliced strawberries and fresh peas or sunflower sprouts.

Kefir Dill Dressing

Janice Innella, The Beauty Chef

This dressing is best served with the Spring Goddess Salad.

1 cup kefir (see note below)
3 tablespoons dill
1 meyer lemon
1 teaspoon ground mustard seed
½ yellow zucchini
1 small piece red onion

Blend all the ingredients and add to the salad before serving.

How to make kefir: ferment 4 young coconuts (including meat and juice) with one packet of Donna Gates Kefir Starter in a high-speed blender. Blend until the mixture becomes a little warm, and then pour into a large gallon-sized jar. Cover and let ferment for at least 36 hours. Once the kefir is ready, you can use it to make the above dressing.

Refrigerate the rest of the kefir to drink at your leisure and watch the beauty start to happen. Be sure to build up slowly to drinking 1 quart a day. When you drink kefir regularly, you will notice that your skin will glow, your nails will become stronger, skin tags will fall off, and liver spots will fade away. Kefir will also help to improve your vision and rebuild your thyroid. This is also a great liver cleanser and has a toning affect on the intestines, even flattening the abdomen. Kefir also has beneficial effects on the endocrine system (adrenals, thyroid, pituitary, ovaries). This is my favorite beauty elixir, as it contains high levels of minerals, including potassium, natural sodium, and magnesium.

Asparagus & Mushroom Salad

Lisa Montgomery

Prep: 40 minutes

Salad
1–2 bunches asparagus, thinly sliced on a diagonal
1 clove garlic, minced
1–2 gala apples, finely chopped
½ cup red onions, finely chopped
1 cup portabella mushrooms, finely sliced
2 tablespoons pine nuts
Sea salt to taste

Dressing
¼-½ cup cold-pressed olive oil
1–2 tablespoons lemon juice
Sea salt and ground pepper to taste

Salad
Cut off the ends of the asparagus and discard. Cut the asparagus diagonally into bite-sized pieces. Toss the asparagus, garlic, apples, onions, portabella mushrooms, pine nuts, and sea salt.

Dressing
Combine all the ingredients in a high-speed blender. Pour over the salad, toss, and serve. You can combine this salad with mixed greens as well.

Tzatziki Greek Dish

Janice Innella, The Beauty Chef

This is a Greek dish made without the dairy. This also makes a great soup, dip, or salad dressing.

Prep: 30 minutes

2 cups raw cashews
2 lemons, juice only
Meat of 2 young Thai coconuts
1 shallot
2 garlic cloves
⅛ teaspoon cayenne pepper
2 cucumbers, peeled, seeded, and chopped
½ teaspoon Celtic sea salt or to taste
½ cup pure water (or more) to taste
1 cup cold-pressed olive oil (or less) to taste
Small bits fresh dill, finely chopped, for garnish

Add all the ingredients (except the cucumbers and dill) to a high-speed blender. Blend until smooth.
Once blended, you can add more water if desired.
Pour dressing over the cucumbers and garnish with fresh dill.

Summertime Curried Corn Salad

Janice Innella, The Beauty Chef

Prep: 30 minutes
Marinate: 2–4 hours

Salad
6–8 ears fresh corn (or 3 cups frozen)
1 small zucchini, diced
1 large red bell pepper, diced
1 bunch scallions, cut into ¼-inch pieces
½ cup Italian parsley, chopped

Dressing
¼ cup organic, unrefined flax or pumpkin seed oil
4 tablespoons raw, organic apple cider vinegar or lemon juice
1 teaspoon curry powder
½ teaspoon sea salt
1–2 cloves garlic, minced

Salad
You can use the corn raw, or blanch it quickly and cool. Combine the raw or cooled corn, zucchini, pepper, scallions, and parsley.

Dressing
Combine the oil, vinegar (or lemon juice), curry powder, sea salt, and garlic.

Combine the vegetables and dressing and marinate for 2–4 hours.

Variation: add 1–2 tablespoons homemade mayonnaise for a creamier dressing.

Denise's Simple Salad

Potlucker Denise Durkin

Prep: 10 minutes

1–2 bags mixed greens

1–3 each assorted vegetables (such as carrot, celery, squash, and
tomatoes), sliced

Lemon-apple cider vinaigrette (enough to lightly cover
vegetables)

Combine all the ingredients and enjoy.

The Essence of Spinach Salad

Joel Odhner, Catalyst Cleanse, Rawlife Line, Philadelphia, PA

This is probably my all-time favorite spinach salad. Joel taught this in one of my very first raw cooking classes, and I have been making it ever since. Whenever I take it to a dinner, it always receives a great review. It is so simple, yet tasty: a true classic. After all these years, I still have not grown tired of it. Joel was one of my first raw teachers. He taught me so much, and I still love making many of the recipes he has shared with me through the years.

Prep: 30 minutes
Soak: 1–2 hours

4 cups spinach
½ teaspoon Celtic sea salt
1 medium avocado, diced
½ cup pine nuts, soaked 1–2 hours, then drained
¼ cup sun-dried tomato, soaked, drained, and finely chopped
¼ cup black olives, pitted and diced
2 tablespoons cold-pressed extra virgin olive oil
2 teaspoons lemon juice

Massage the spinach with sea salt until moist. Add all the remaining ingredients, mix well, and serve.

Chopped Fall Fitness Salad with Spicy Vinaigrette

Janice Innella, The Beauty Chef

Janice's salads are always light and refreshing with twists for your palate. She is one of the best raw chefs I have met. Plus, she's also a sweetheart.

Prep: 30 minutes

Salad
1 head fennel
4 scallions
2 carrots
1 zucchini
2 red peppers, finely chopped
2 cups parsley
1 cup pumpkin seeds (½ cup ground)
1 avocado, chopped into cubes
1 bunch pea sprouts
1 cup raw cashews, chopped slightly
Juice of 1 lime
1 pear to garnish

Vinaigrette
1 tablespoon nama shoyu or wheat-free tamari
½ cup toasted sesame oil
1 tablespoon pumpkin seeds
Juice of 2 limes
1 small piece ginger
2 red chilis or 2 tablespoons chilli paste
2 tablespoons agave nectar
Pinch sea salt
1 cup pure water

Salad
Chop the fennel, scallion, carrots, zucchini, pepper, and 1 cup of parsley in a food processor. Pour into a bowl and set aside.

Add the remaining ingredients and toss with the first bowl.

Vinaigrette
Combine all the ingredients in a high-speed blender. Pour over salad, toss, and serve. Garnish with the pear.

Tropical Applesauce

Lisa Montgomery

This is a simple and easy recipe, and it tastes so good.

Prep: 15 minutes

2 apples, cored and peeled
1 banana
1 mango, cored and peeled
Water, to thin
1 tablespoon shredded, dried coconut

Combine all the ingredients in a food processor to desired consistency and serve. If you wish to thin the applesauce, add water to desired consistency. Stir in dried coconut by hand.

You can also add cinnamon and/or raisins to taste. If you want to increase the amount that you wish to make, just increase the quantity, keeping the same proportions (for example, 2 to 2 or 3 to 3).

Harvest Salad

Lisa Montgomery

I created this recipe when I was asked to do a book signing/demo at the Phoenixville, PA, Farmer's Market. The stipulation was I had to use ingredients that were in season at the market and complete the dish without using any electricity (the market is held outside, and electricity is not available).

I thought for a few minutes and came up with the following recipe. Ironically—and/or divinely—it was a huge hit at the market. They loved the colors and freshness. Believe it or not, you do not have to be a raw gourmet chef to prepare good food. I am reiterating how simple raw recipes can be. All that you need to do is think about what you like, what is available, what you are in the mood for, and then put it together.

Red beets, peeled into spirals, to taste
Sweet potato or yams, peeled into spirals, to taste
Apples, cored and diced, to taste
Peaches (and/or pears), cored and diced, to taste
Raisins to taste

Combine all the ingredients in a bowl and serve: it is that simple.

Tropical Harvest Salad

Lisa Montgomery

Red beets, peeled into spirals, to taste
Sweet potato or yams, peeled into spirals, to taste
Apples, cored and diced, to taste
Peaches (and/or pears), cored and diced, to taste
Raisins to taste
Coconut, shredded, to taste
Pineapple, chopped, to taste

Combine all the ingredients in a bowl and serve.

Pineapple Salsa

*I saw a recipe for pineapple salsa somewhere, and wrote down what I
wanted in my own variation, shown here. You can use this recipe for
guidance and put in your own salsa what works for you.*

Pineapple chunks to taste
Red pepper, finely chopped, to taste
Red onion, finely chopped, to taste
Green pepper, finely chopped, to taste
Raw honey to taste
Sea salt and pepper to taste

Combine all the ingredients in a bowl, serve, and eat.

Fennel Orange Salad

Lisa Montgomery

This recipe was inspired by a knife class that I took during night class at my local high school.

Prep: 15–20 minutes

Orange slices to taste
Fennel, shredded and chopped into bite-sized pieces, to taste
Cold-pressed olive oil to taste
Apple cider vinegar or lemon juice to taste
Sea salt and pepper to taste

Combine all the ingredients in a bowl. Toss, serve, and eat.

Cranberry Relish

Potlucker Peggy O'Neil

Prep: 20–30 minutes
Refrigerate: overnight or a few hours

1 (16 oz.) package fresh cranberries, washed
1½ cups raisins, un-soaked (they will absorb the orange juice)
2 oranges, rinds, seeds, and white membranes removed, cut into
      sections
2 apples, cored and diced (pared or un-pared)
Sea salt to taste

Combine all the ingredients in a food processor until everything is about the same size. Mix together and refrigerate for several hours or overnight

Watermelon Salad with Basil

Lisa Montgomery

This is my own adaptation of J. M. Hirsch's (AP Food Editor) salad with meat. I obviously have removed the meat.

Prep: 15 minutes
Servings: 6

6 cups watermelon, cut
2 cups fresh strawberries, quartered
2 green apples, cored and diced
1 tablespoon cold-pressed extra virgin olive oil
1 tablespoon lemon juice
½ teaspoon sea salt
¼ teaspoon ground black pepper
¼ cup fresh basil, finely chopped

In a large bowl, combine the watermelon, strawberries, and apples. Set aside.

In a small bowl, whisk together the cold-pressed olive oil, lemon juice, salt, and pepper. Drizzle the mixture over the fruit. Gently toss to combine. Scatter the basil over the salad. Serve immediately at room temperature.

If you like, you could also add diced fresh cantaloupe to this salad. The original recipe called for cooked bacon for a nice crunch. To keep the crunch, you could add soaked, dehydrated, and finely chopped sesame seeds, pine nuts, or walnuts. Ground pumpkin seeds would also be really nice on this salad. I have even been known to finely chop macadamia nuts and sprinkle them over the top, as well. You can see how just changing the nut can make this salad come out differently, so do not get locked into thinking that you need to have specific ingredients on hand; just substitute something else. You could even try grating raw cacao over the top of this salad, as well. As you can tell, I can get carried away with all of the possibilities. It happens a lot; I am a foodie, after all.

Corn & Blueberry Salad

Potlucker Peggy O'Neill

I tried to takes notes as I put this together, but I did not actually measure anything. That would take the fun out of summer salads. They are never the same twice at my house. I often add chopped red bell pepper and celery. You can substitute lime juice (and zest) for the vinegar, or add cardamom or marjoram. Enjoy!

6 ears fresh corn, cut from the cob
1 pint blueberries
Generous slice of onion (or scallions)
¼ cup apple cider vinegar
2–3 tablespoons honey
Fresh mint to taste
Fresh thyme or oregano to taste

Combine corn and blueberries in a bowl and set aside.

Chop or process together the mint, thyme (or oregano), and onion (or scallions), and then add it to corn and blueberries.

Stir together the apple cider vinegar and honey. Add salt and pepper to taste, and blend all together for your dressing. Pour the dressing over the corn, blueberries, mint, thyme/oregano, and onion/scallions.

Alorah's Mediterranean Avocado Salad

Alorah Arliotis (www.thewiserwoman.co.uk), Glastonbury, England

Remember, avocadoes are fruit!

Prep: 25 minutes

3 avocados
½ cucumber
1 red pepper, chopped and cubed
3 spring onions, chopped
½ cup fresh cilantro or coriander, chopped
1 teaspoon paprika
½ teaspoon salt (or to taste)
1 teaspoon dry/dehydrated kelp flakes (optional)
3 green olives, pitted and chopped
1 small clove garlic, chopped
2 lemons, juiced
½ cup olive oil

Scoop the meat out of the avocado and place in a bowl. Mash the avocados roughly and leave chunky. Peel and cube the cucumber, then chop the red pepper into similar sized cubes. Trim and chop the onions. Set aside some of the greens from onions.

Combine all of the ingredients one by one into the avocado, adding the lemon and oil last. Do not mash the avocado, but fold gently. Add the lemon and oil last. Garnish with spring onion greens.

Let salad stand for 20 minutes before serving. This salad will keep for up to two days in an air-tight container. To help preserve your salad, place the avocado stone in the center of your salad and sprinkle with extra lemon juice before storing.

Hearty Fall Fruit Salad
Tonya Zavasta (www.BeautifulOnRaw.com)

Tonya has written numerous books such as Your Right to Be Beautiful *and* 100 Days to 100 Percent Raw

Servings: approximately 4
Soak: 2–4 hours (walnuts)
Prep: 30 minutes

2 lemons
2 oranges
2 sweet potatoes, peeled and grated
2 apples, grated
2 tablespoons ginger root, grated
1 cup walnuts, soaked, rinsed, and chopped
Meat of 1 young Thai coconut
1 cup pineapple, chopped
Handful of raisins
Cinnamon to taste

Juice the lemons and oranges. Set aside.

Combine the sweet potatoes, apples, and ginger in a serving bowl.

Add the walnuts, coconut meat, pineapple, and raisins. Toss together with the juice and serve with a dusting of cinnamon on top.

Tropical Salad

Linda Cooper, Linda Louise Cakes, Harleysville, PA

Prep: 15–20 minutes

½ large ripe red papaya, peeled and seeded
1–2 mangos, peeled and pitted
2 bananas, peeled
4 leaves romaine lettuce, shredded

Combine the papaya, mangoes, and bananas in a food processor and pulse until chopped, but not pureed. Pour over a bed of shredded romaine lettuce. Mix together and enjoy.

Avocado Corn Salad

Potlucker Nancy Sydlosky

Prep: 20 minutes

2 avocadoes, diced
2 ears fresh corn, cut from the cob
2 tomatoes, diced
½ red onion, finely chopped
2 tablespoons fresh lime juice
2 tablespoons cold-pressed olive oil
Sea salt to taste

Mix all the ingredients together in a bowl and serve. It is that simple.

Bok Choy Delight

Lisa Montgomery

Prep: 30 minutes

2 pounds bok choy, finely sliced
1–2 cups shitake mushrooms, finely sliced and stems removed
1 tablespoon cold-pressed olive oil
1 tablespoons Austria's Finest, Naturally pumpkin seed oil
1 teaspoon toasted sesame oil
1 cup broccoli florets
1 orange, sliced
⅛ teaspoon fresh ginger, grated
1–2 tablespoons wheat-free tamari
1 red pepper, finely chopped
2 cloves garlic, minced
Sea salt and pepper to taste

Mix all the ingredients in a bowl and serve.

Broccoli Salad

Pat Umble, Certified Raw Food Teacher

Pat holds a Master's degree in holistic nutrition. She co-hosts a monthly raw food potluck in Lancaster County, PA.

This is my all-time favorite broccoli salad. Whenever I make this salad and take it to an event, it is always a big hit. The good news is, besides being tasty, it is also quick and easy to make.

Prep: 20–30 minutes

Salad
5 cups broccoli, chopped
1–2 carrots, shredded (optional)
½ cup sunflower seeds or raw slivered almonds
½ cup raisins, soaked for fifteen minutes

Dressing
1 cup raw cashews, soaked for one hour (or you can use
        almonds that have been soaked 8 hours)
2 tablespoons agave
2 tablespoons raw apple cider vinegar or fresh lemon juice
2 tablespoons red onion, finely chopped
½ teaspoon salt
¼ cup water

Salad
Mix all the ingredients in a bowl.

Dressing
Blend all the ingredients in a high-speed blender and pour over the broccoli. If you prefer a lot of dressing with your salads (like I do), you can easily double the dressing recipe.

Tex-Mex Rico Rolls

Karmyn Malone (www.KarmynMalone.com)

Prep: 30–40 minutes
Yield: 24 rolls (serves 2–4 people)

2 Hass avocados
2 medium to large cucumbers
2 Roma tomatoes
Cilantro or coriander
3 scallions (green part only)
4 sheets raw nori
Ground dried chipotle pepper or cayenne pepper, to taste
      (optional)

Preparation

Cut the avocados in half lengthwise. Remove seed and discard. Slice avocados lengthwise. Each half should have around four slices. Set aside.

Using a vegetable peeler, peel skin off the cucumbers. Discard skin. With the peeler, continue to thinly peel cucumbers lengthwise all around until you reach the seeds. Discard seeded portion or enjoy at another time.

Thinly slice the tomatoes lengthwise into strips, omitting seeds and juice. Set aside. Rinse cilantro/coriander and scallions. Set aside. Set aside 4 sheets of raw nori.

Assembly

On each sheet of raw nori, spread half an avocado's worth of slices. Sprinkle chipotle pepper or cayenne pepper on top of avocado (more or less to taste). Add a layer of thinly sliced cucumber (½ cucumber's worth) on top of avocado. Add a layer of Roma tomato slices (½ tomato's worth. Add a layer of cilantro/coriander (more or less to taste). Add one scallion. Now you're ready to roll. Before making the rolls, make sure to lightly moisten each end (I find that using a cut tomato to moisten both ends helps the roll to stay together much better). Roll the vegetables to the other end. Make sure that the nori is completely wrapped. Cut the nori roll into six portions. I recommend that you first cut the roll in half and then cut each half in thirds. Arrange on a platter and repeat the assembly three more times. Serve immediately.

Fiesta Cabbage

Lisa Montgomery

Prep: 25 minutes

Cabbage
1 cup shredded red cabbage
1 cup shredded green cabbage
¼ cup red onion, finely diced
2 scallions, finely sliced
1–2 medium tomato, chopped

Dressing
2 soaked sundried tomatoes
⅛ cup red onion
2 tablespoons cold-pressed olive oil
¼ teaspoon curry
¼ teaspoon cumin
1 tablespoon agave

Cabbage
Shred the cabbages using the "S" blade in your food processor and set aside in a bowl. Combine the red onion, scallions, and tomato with the shredded cabbage and set aside.

Dressing
Combine the dressing ingredients in a high-speed blender and pour over Fiesta Cabbage and blend with your hands thoroughly. You can eat as a side dish, add on top of a salad, or add to a wrap whether it be a seed/flax wrap or romaine/collard leaf wrap. You can also warm the Fiesta Cabbage by placing in a glass bowl and setting the Tribest Sedona Dehydrator to 105°F for 30 minutes or until desired temperature.

Unroasted Brussels Sprouts

Lisa Montgomery

I created this recipe after eating at Zaytinya Restaurant in Washington, DC. I wanted a raw salad that tasted like roasted vegetables, which was one of their specialties. You can also make this salad by replacing the Brussels sprouts with cauliflower.

Whenever I serve this dish, everyone cannot believe that the vegetables are not roasted. So, when you feel like you need the emotional comfort of cooked food, but want to still eat raw, this is a dish that will not only captivate your taste buds, but will meet your emotional needs, as well.

Prep: 20–30 minutes
Dehydrator: 2–4 hours

Brussels sprouts, sliced in half
2–3 tablespoon pine nuts
2–3 tablespoon capers
2–3 tablespoon raisins
1–2 tablespoons raw agave
1–2 tablespoons cold-pressed olive oil
Sea salt and cracked ground black pepper (or freshly ground
        green, black, red, and white peppers) to taste

Mix all the ingredients together in a bowl, using enough agave and cold-pressed olive oil to make sure that your Brussels sprouts are totally covered (I have also been known to add 1 or 2 teaspoons of lemon juice). Place in a glass baking dish, and then place in your dehydrator for 2–4 hours.

Curry Carrot Salad

Joel Odhner, Catalyst Cleanse, Rawlife Line, Philadelphia, PA

The flavors of cumin and curry add a unique flavor to an old-time favorite dish. Bring this salad to your next picnic for a new delight for all to enjoy.

Prep: 20–30 minutes

Sauce
1 cup Brazil nuts
1 cup water
½ cup cold-pressed olive oil
1 tablespoon curry
1 tablespoon cumin

Salad
3 cups carrots, shredded
½ cup raisins
1 cup celery, diced
1 red onion, diced

Sauce
Place all the ingredients in a high-powered blender and blend until smooth.

Salad
Fold sauce into the remaining ingredients. Lasts 3–4 days, refrigerated (if you have not already eaten it up by then).

Creamy Cashew Yogurt with Vegetables
Potlucker Ed Tabas

When Ed brought this recipe to my raw potluck he also performed his original song Chew Your Food Up A Little Bit Longer, *which was a big hit with those in attendance.*

Prep: 12–24 hours (yogurt), 20–30 minutes (vegetables)

Cashew Yogurt
3 cups raw cashews
1 capsule acidophilus (Kyo-Dophilus® brand is the best)
2–3 cups filtered water (or enough to cover the cashews, so the
    blender can circulate)

Vegetables
Baby spinach to taste
Spring mix to taste
Tomatoes, sliced or diced, to taste
Sweet onion, diced, to taste
Jicama, peeled and diced, to taste
Garlic to taste
Basil to taste
Parsley to taste
Dill to taste
Dulse to taste
Sea salt and black pepper to taste

Cashew Yogurt
Blend all the ingredients in a high-speed blender until they become silky smooth (no grit). Place in a container with a loose lid and leave in a warm space for 12–24 hours, so fermentation can take

place. Make sure that you leave enough space in your container, so the cashew yogurt can rise.

Vegetables
Prepare all the ingredients and toss together in a bowl with the cashew yogurt.

By now, you may have realized that preparing raw foods typically does not require you to measure so precisely like you would in standard American cooking. For example, the above salad calls for basil, parsley, and dill. So, if you do not have parsley or if you hate the taste of parsley, you can easily make the salad without parsley or throw in another herb, instead.

Mexican Corn Salad

Joel Odhner, Catalyst Cleanse, Rawlife Line, Philadelphia, PA

Prep: 20–30 minutes

2 cups fresh organic corn kernels
1 cup red pepper, chopped
¼ cup scallions, chopped
¼ cup fresh cilantro, finely chopped
2 tablespoons lemon juice
2 tablespoons cold-pressed extra virgin olive oil
½ teaspoon ground cumin
Sea salt to taste

Combine all the ingredients in a bowl, toss, and eat.

Tater Salad with Honey Lemon Dill Sauce

Eric Rivkin, Founding member of Jewel of the Sun (a sustainable community in Costa Rica) and founder of the non-profit Viva La Raw Project, dedicated to health and nutrition education for the masses.

Soak: nuts, 5–6 hours
Prep: 30 minutes
Serves 10–12

Salad
3 pounds jicama, peeled and diced into ¼-inch cubes (or spiral
    sliced with a Spirooli Spiralizer into curls)
3 celery stalks, sliced thin diagonally
1 red bell pepper, finely diced
2 ears fresh sweet corn kernels
1 medium zucchini, diced or julienned into thin strips
¼ cup fresh dill, coarsely chopped
¼ cup fresh chives, finely chopped

Honey Lemon Dill Sauce
½ cup raw pine nuts, soaked 5–6 hours and rinsed (or
    macadamias)
Juice of 1 lemon
Juice of 1 orange
2 tablespoons raw honey or 2 pitted dates
2 tablespoons fresh dill, minced
½ teaspoon turmeric

Salad
Toss the salad ingredients together by hand, and then toss the salad with the Honey Lemon Dill Sauce.

Honey Lemon Dill Sauce

Blend the ingredients in a high-speed blender until creamy. Pour the dressing over the salad ingredients and mix gently.

To serve, arrange several large, clean leaves of Napa cabbage or red-leaf lettuce in a large serving bowl, and add salad-sauce mix. Garnish with more sprigs of dill, paprika, edible flowers, chives, and/or chive flowers.

Mashed Taters

Joel Odhner, Catalyst Cleanse, Rawlife Line, Philadelphia, PA

I must confess that one of the standard American dishes I actually do miss is my Mom's homemade mashed potatoes. In fact, once we found that I was allergic to dairy, she made her mashed potatoes with potato water, and they were still just as good. Since my Mom has passed, and I am seeking a healthier alternative to mashed potatoes (a major comfort food for me), Joel's "Mashed Taters" help to fill the potato void.

1 head cauliflower, chopped
1 cup raw cashews
½ cup cold-pressed olive oil
1–2 cloves garlic
Salt and pepper to taste

Place all the ingredients in food processor and blend until smooth.

Miso Gravy

Janice Innella, The Beauty Chef

Janice's Miso Gravy will go nicely with Joel's Mashed Taters.
Notice that I am not giving up my mashed potatoes and gravy fix. I am
just doing it in a healthier way.

Prep: 15–20 minutes

6 tablespoons white or red miso
1 cup raw cashews
½ red onion, chopped
½ teaspoon white pepper
Dash of black pepper
1 teaspoon Celtic sea salt or umeboshi plum paste
⅛ teaspoon cayenne pepper
Agave nectar, to taste
2 cups pure water
½ cup zucchini, chopped
½ cup carrots, chopped

Blend all together to a creamy consistency in a high-speed blender.

You can put both your "Mashed Taters" and "Miso Gravy" in glass bowls, and warm in a dehydrator. That way you can serve them warm.

Portabella Mushroom Marinade

Loreta Vainus, Loreta's Living Foods

Be sure to contact Loreta for her new DVD, Grow Your Own Greens. *Loreta was also one of my first teachers and is a wealth of information regarding growing wheat grass and sprouts.*

Prep: 15 minutes
Marinate: 2 hours

2 lemons, juiced
1 orange, juiced
¼ cup cold-pressed olive oil
3 cloves garlic
1 tablespoon Braggs apple cider vinegar
1–2 tablespoons basil, parsley, or oregano

Combine all of the ingredients in a bowl and pour over the portabella mushrooms. Let stand for a couple of hours.

I have a plastic marinater from Tupperware that makes marinating mushrooms and vegetables easy. You place everything in the marinater, and then you can turn it over every so often, depending on the dish.

Growing mushrooms is on my list of things that I want to do someday. I am looking forward to attempting to grow my own mushrooms next year. Gardener's Supply has several kits for growing your own mushrooms.

Please visit my website, www.livingdynamically.com, and check out my raised-bed heirloom organic garden.

Sea Veggie Salad

Elaina Love, author of Elaina's Pure Joy Kitchen *(www.PureJoyLove. com), (520) 394-0123. Elaina is a raw food chef and teacher. She also certifies up-and-coming raw food chefs.*
Ocean vegetables, like those in this recipe, greatly enhance the functioning of the immune system. They are also rich in minerals and help strengthen the thyroid.

Makes 1 pint
Prep: 25 minutes
Serves: 4

½ cup arame, dry
2 tablespoons flax oil
1–5 tablespoons lemon juice (1½ lemons)
3 scallions or ¼ red onion, shredded
¼–½ teaspoon Celtic sea salt

Cover the arame with purified water and let soak for 15 minutes.

Mix all ingredients together and let marinate an hour or more (overnight is best as the flavors have time to meld and the sea vegetable flavor mellows).

If you don't have time to marinade, omit or lessen the amount of onions.

Combine the ingredients in a mixing bowl. Place in a glass dish and dehydrate for 30 minutes to warm.

Sprouted Quinoa Breakfast Cereal

Loreta Vainus, Loreta's Living Foods

Be sure to contact Loreta for her new DVD, Grow Your Own Greens.

Prep: 20 minutes (plus 2 days sprouting time)

½ cup quinoa
1 cup fresh organic strawberry
1 tablespoon flax seeds (not soaked)
½ cup water (or coconut water)

Soak ½ cup dried quinoa in clean, purified water for 6 to 8 hours. Place the soaked quinoa into a nylon sprout bag and sprout for 2 days, rinsing 2–3 times per day (morning and evening).

Place all the ingredients in a Vitamix® blender and blend well.

Note: Before adding the sprouted quinoa to the blender, be sure to rinse the quinoa several times before preparing your breakfast cereal.

Variation: Blend with papaya, blueberries, dates, bananas, stevia (powder or fresh stevia leaves), mint leaves, and/or cinnamon. If you want to serve this at lunch or dinner, serve over greens.

Rainbow Raw Rice
Potlucker Grace Culbertson

Prep: 30 minutes

2 cups cauliflower
2 cups jicama, peeled and sliced
¼ red onion
¼ cup raw corn, cut from cob
¼ cup raw peas, from pod
1 carrot, grated
½–1 cup cold-pressed olive oil
½ cup pumpkin or sunflower seeds (soaked in Bragg's Liquid
      Amino and dehydrated)
1 or 2 pinches sea salt (if needed, to taste)

Chop 2 cups of cauliflower in food processor until gritty. Remove and place in mixing bowl. Chop peeled jicama in food processor briefly, so it does not become too liquefied, but is in small bite-sized pieces, and place in bowl with cauliflower. Add sliced or finely chopped onion and fresh corn, peas, and grated carrot. Pour in your favorite cold-pressed olive oil and mix. Lastly, add sunflower seeds or pumpkin seeds that have been soaked in Bragg's Liquid Amino and toss with large wooden spoons.

Bubbie's Sauerkraut Red Cabbage Combo

Loreta Vainus, Loreta's Living Foods

Be sure to contact Loreta for her new DVD, Grow Your Own Greens.

Prep: 30 minutes
Let Stand: 5 days

1 jar Bubbie's Sauerkraut
2 heads red cabbage
1 red onion
2 tablespoons caraway seeds

Remove the outer leaves of the red cabbage and reserve them to line your crock. Shred the cabbage finely. Shred the onion finely. Combine the Bubbie's sauerkraut with the red cabbage, onion, and caraway seeds. Place the sauerkraut into a crock, cover, and let stand for 5 days.

Mango Tomato Salad

Karmyn Malone (www.KarmynMalone.com)

Prep: 20 minutes

2 large mangoes, diced and pitted
4 Roma tomatoes, diced
1 cup cilantro, chopped
3 slices red onion, finely chopped
1 tomatillo, diced (make sure to remove white part and discard)
2 slices jalapeño peppers, finely chopped to taste
1 lemon or lime, juiced
1 cucumber, peeled and diced

Mix all ingredients in a large bowl and enjoy.

Wild Rice Salad

Lisa Montgomery

In case you are tired of green-based salads, this Wild Rice Salad is a great side salad.

Sprout: 24–36 hours

¼–½ cup wild rice
Water to cover
Assorted vegetables (see note below)
Sea salt to taste

Place wild rice in a glass jar, cover with water, place in your dehydrator, and let "bloom" for 24–36 hours. You know your rice is ready to go when all of the rice "blooms" or "pops." Make sure that the rice is covered with water. Make sure that you leave enough room in the jar for the rice to expand. Once the rice has "bloomed," rinse and set aside. You can use this basic rice in many dishes, and, by changing up the ingredients, you can make it Mexican, Japanese, or whatever you prefer.

Here is my favorite flavor combination for this rice:

Scallions, finely chopped
Shitake mushrooms, washed with moist paper towel, stems removed, and discarded (or feed to your chickens)
Carrots, finely sliced or julienned
Juice of 1 lemon

Toasted sesame oil to taste
Garlic cloves, finely chopped, to taste
Wheat-free tamari
Austria's Finest, Naturally raw pumpkin seed oil
Fresh peas (when in season)

If you want a Mexican flavor, you can add Mexican chili powder and tomatoes.

Sauerkraut

Linda Cooper, Linda Louise Cakes, Harleysville, PA

Prep: 20 minutes
Stand Time: 4–7 days

2 heads green cabbage
2 heads purple cabbage

Peel off the outer leaves from the cabbage and put aside. Chop the cabbage into pieces, and process in a food processor in batches until finely ground. Put the ground cabbage into a stainless steel or glass bowl, and pack down. Cover with the outer cabbage leaves. Put a plate on top of the cabbage leaves (this should fit nicely in the bowl without leaving much, if any, space between it and the edge of the bowl). Place a filled, gallon-sized jug on top of the plate. Cover everything with a towel. Let sit like this at room temperature for 4–7 days. The cabbage will ferment in its own juices, which should be present on top. Taste to determine when ready. Good sauerkraut will taste "zingy." When ready, peel off the whole cabbage leaves and skim off a small layer underneath. Place in a glass container and store in a refrigerator. Can be stored for several months in a glass, sealed container in a refrigerator.

You can use any combination of green and purple cabbage for this recipe.

Simple Spinach Salad

Mindy Marcozzi, Agape Health & Yoga

Prep: 15–20 minutes

Salad
2 bags fresh spinach
Fresh strawberries, sliced
Handful of raw pine nuts

Ranch Dressing
1 cup raw cashews
½ teaspoon onion powder
Spring water
1 teaspoon dill
½ teaspoon garlic powder
Celtic or pink sea salt to taste

Salad
Combine the spinach, sliced strawberries, and pine nuts in a bowl. Toss with the dressing, or serve the dressing in a pretty dish and allow guests to put the dressing on their own salad. If you are making this recipe for yourself, keep the dressing in a separate container, and that way, when you pack it in your lunch each day, you can put the dressing on when you are ready to eat the salad. That way, the salad will not wilt.

Ranch Dressing
Mix the ingredients in a high-speed blender. Add enough water so the dressing is creamy and smooth. If you want a thick dressing or dip, use less water. If you want a thinner consistency, add more water. The great thing is you do not have to be a brain surgeon to make raw foods or this dressing. You can see how versatile this dressing is.

Tangy Raw Cauliflower Salad
Potlucker Denise Durkin

Prep: 20 minutes

Salad
1 small head cauliflower, broken into small, bite-sized pieces
½ large red onion, diced
3 large carrots, shredded

Dressing
2 cups fresh basil leaves
1 large juicy tomato
½ cup sun-dried tomatoes
¼ cup cold-pressed olive oil
Juice of 2 lemons
½ teaspoon fresh ground pepper

Salad
In a bowl, combine cauliflower, red onion, and carrots. Set aside.

Dressing
Combine the dressing ingredients in a high-speed blender. Pour dressing over salad, toss, and enjoy.

Tip from Lisa: Sun-Dried Tomatoes

I make my own sun-dried tomatoes in my Sonoma Tribest dehydrator. When my tomatoes come in season, one of the ways that I harvest them, besides popping them in my mouth, is to slice them thinly, place on the racks of my Sonoma Dehydrator, and dehydrate them until dry. I store the tomatoes in air-tight, zip-lock bags. When using vacuum-seal bags, I actually double bag them. If you do not, the bugs can eat through the bags. They like the tomatoes, too. I am selfish: I do not want to share with the bugs.

Simple Zucchini Salad
Potlucker Deb Rockwell

Actually, I call it a raw version of Surf and Turf.

Salad
Spiralized zucchini (turf)
Kelp noodles (surf)
Chopped tomatoes

Pesto Dressing
Fresh basil
Pine nuts and olive oil
Kelp granules for garnish (optional)

Salad
Spiralize the zucchini and place kelp noodles in a bowl.

Pesto Dressing
Combine the pesto ingredients in a food processor.

   Toss the pesto with the zucchini and kelp. Finish the dish with chopped tomatoes (red and yellow), and sprinkle kelp granules on to taste for a finishing touch.

Southwestern Stuffed Avocadoes

Sheryl Chavarria, owner of Raw Can Roll Café and Pure Body Spa in Douglassville, PA

Prep: 30 minutes
Dehydrate: 5–6 hours (+ 20 minutes)

2 avocados
6 grape or cherry tomatoes, halved
½ cucumber, peeled and chopped into small pieces
½–1 clove garlic, pressed
1 tablespoon lime or lemon juice
1 teaspoon chili powder
½ teaspoon cumin powder
Salt to taste (approximately ½ teaspoon)
Pinch cayenne

Slice avocados in half and deseed (keeping the skin intact).

Take a large spoon and scoop out the avocado pulp. Set skins aside. Cut avocado into meduim chunks. Mix in all the other ingredients and mash lightly. Spoon the mixture into avocado skins, and eat.

You might think that this does not sound like a lot to eat as a "Main Event" of a meal, but the avocados are extremely filling. You could eat a couple of these on some greens and be stuffed–like an avocado. That was a "Raw Garden" joke.

Spaghetti alla Puttanesca, Alfredo, or Pink Sauce with Parmesan Cheese

Sheryll Chavarria, Pure Body Spa & Raw Can Roll Café, Douglassville, PA

Sheryll taught us this recipe in a raw cooking class and it is to die for. You can choose to serve the pasta with the puttanesca, alfredo, or pink sauce. Then top with Parmesan cheese.

Spaghetti
Prep: 15 minutes

Puttanesca Sauce
Prep: 20 minutes
Yields: 4

Alfredo Sauce
Prep: 15 minutes

Spaghetti
4 zucchini, peeled (spiralized or shredded with a vegetable
        peeler)
1 lemon, juiced

Puttanesca Sauce
1 red bell pepper, chopped
5 tomatoes, chopped (preferably plum or Roma)
Handful sun-dried tomatoes (to create medium thickness),
        optional
Bunch fresh basil, oregano, parsley
Thyme and rosemary (optional)
Pinch cayenne pepper or finely chopped hot peppers
2 cloves garlic, minced

Celtic sea salt to taste or 2 tablespoons white mello miso
½ cup black olives, sliced
¼ cup olive oil, adder after sauce is prepared

Alfredo Sauce
1½ cups raw pine nuts, soaked
1½ cups raw cashews, soaked
2 cloves garlic, minced
2 tablespoons lemon, juiced
½ cup water (add more if necessary)
Celtic sea salt to taste

Parmesan Cheese
1 cup sesame seeds, soaked
1 tablespoon fresh parsley, finely chopped
Pinch Celtic sea salt

Spaghetti
After zucchini is prepared, place in bowl. Pour lemon juice on zucchini and work through well (tossing carefully so as not to break the zucchini). The lemon works to break down the zucchini so it becomes softer. You may place the zucchini (pasta) and the sauce in a dehydrator for about 1 hour to warm.

Puttanesca Sauce
Combine all the ingredients (except olive oil) in blender until smooth (or chunky if you prefer). If sauce is not thick enough, add more sun-dried tomatoes. Place in serving bowl, then add olive oil and stir. Do not blend olive oil in blender. To make a chunkier sauce, you may put all the ingredients into a food processor instead of using a blender. Serve on top of zucchini or summer squash spaghetti.

Alfredo Sauce
Combine all ingredients together in a high-speed blender until smooth. Serve on top of zucchini or summer squash spaghetti.

Pink Sauce
Combine ¾ parts alfredo sauce to ¼ part puttanesca sauce. Mix both together and serve on top of zucchini or summer squash spaghetti.

Parmesan Cheese
Finely grind sesame seeds in coffee grinder. In a small bowl, add the rest of the ingredients and mix well. Serve on top of pasta dish.

Spaghetti with Sausage and Peppers

Barbara Shevkun, Rawfully Tempting

Barbara is an upcoming star who has her own raw product line and is a great teacher.

Prep: 60 minutes

Veggie Marinade
1 large tomato
¼ red or orange bell pepper
½ cup onion, chopped
1 tablespoon olive oil
1 teaspoon each fresh basil, parsley, dried oregano (or to taste)
Pinch cayenne pepper
Pinch sea salt

Veggies
1 red bell pepper, sliced thin
1 orange bell pepper, sliced thin
½ large onion, sliced thin
½–1 cup mushrooms, sliced
½ zucchini, sliced thin

Spaghetti
½ package kelp noodles (kelp noodles come in 12-ounce
        packages)
Zucchini, spiralized (1 zucchini per person)

Veggie Marinade
Blend ingredients until smooth. Set aside.

   A sneaky way to add more greens into your family's diet is to add a bit of chopped kale to the marinade as well.

Veggies

Place all sliced vegetables in a large bowl and mix with marinade. Let sit for at least 1 hour. Spread on a non-stick dehydrator sheet and dehydrate at 110°F for two hours, mixing and stirring halfway through).

Spaghetti

Rinse kelp noodles and cut in half. Soak in warm lemon water at least 1 hour or more, while preparing the rest of your meal. Spiralize zucchini shortly before serving and let sit in a strainer to remove some of the excess liquid.

Rawfully Tempting Marinara Sauce and Rawsages

Rawsages are optional in this dish, but add a wonderful texture and flavor.

Marinara Sauce
3 tomatoes
½ cup kale, chopped
1 clove garlic, chopped
¼ red onion
¼ red or orange bell pepper
½ avocado
2 teaspoon lemon juice
Fresh basil, to taste
Sea salt, to taste
Cayenne pepper, to taste
Pinch of dried oregano

Rawsages (optional)
¾ cup walnuts (soak overnight, towel dry, may dehydrate a bit)
¼ cup pecans (soak overnight, towel dry, may dehydrate a bit)
Dash crushed red pepper
2 medjool dates, pitted and chopped
½ teaspoon fennel seeds, crushed or ground
Dash cayenne
¼ teaspoon each salt, pepper, oregano, basil, sage, thyme

Marinara Sauce
Blend ingredients. Taste and season to your liking. Set aside.

Rawsages

Process the nuts until well chopped in a food processor. Add remaining ingredients, and process until it begins to come together but still has texture.

Roll into small balls and dehydrate at 110°F for 6–8 hours. To store, freeze in an air-tight container and use for raw pizzas and other Italian-style dishes.

Assembly

Place a mixture of kelp and zucchini noodles on each plate. Top with marinated veggies. Add marinara sauce and garnish with rawsages and chopped fresh parsley or basil.

You can warm veggies and marinara in dehydrator prior to serving.

You can serve this as an amazing Main Event or make each of it in parts and combine with other dishes . . . Mix it up.

Vegetable Chow Mein

Potlucker Cat Janson

Prep: 20 minutes

Butternut squash, chopped
Yellow squash, sliced
Zucchini, spiralized
Shitake mushrooms, de-stemmed and chopped
Grated ginger
Nama shoyu (I use wheat-free tamari)
Green onions, finely sliced
Cold-pressed olive oil
Cilantro leaves, chopped, to taste

Combine the ingredients, toss, and serve.

Seasoned Austria's Finest Pumpkin Seeds

Lisa Montgomery

Makes 2 cups or 8 servings
Prep: 10 minutes
Dehydrate: 24 hours

2 cups Austria's Finest, Naturally pumpkin seeds
2 tablespoons wheat-free tamari
1 teaspoon onion powder
1 teaspoon garlic powder

Combine all the ingredients and mix well. Place on a Teflex-lined dehydrator tray and dehydrate at 105°F for 24 hours or until crisp. Store in an air-tight container in the refrigerator.

I would recommend doubling or tripling this recipe if you want to make sure that you have enough for the quinoa recipe above. The reason is they are a great snack, and I tend to eat them a lot. This is also a great recipe just to have in ball jars on your counter or in a Ziploc bag/Tupperware container in your car so you always have a healthy snack handy.

Eggplant and Spinach Parmesan

Barbara Shevkun, Rawfully Tempting

Prep: This is one of those dishes you want to make on a Saturday . . . all day

Eggplant
2 small eggplants, peeled and sliced thinly (I use one white
　　eggplant and one graffiti eggplant. They are small and
　　very tender)

Coating
¼ cup pine nuts
¾ cup raw almonds
Dried Italian herbs, to taste
Sea salt, to taste

Cheese
½ cup cashews
½ cup macadamia nuts
1–2 tablespoon lemon juice
Onion powder, to taste
½ garlic clove, crushed
Sea salt, to taste
Water to blend
3–4 cups fresh spinach, chopped
Your favorite marinara sauce (I suggest using Barbara's
　　Marinara Sauce on page 111)

Sauce
2–3 large tomatoes
1 clove garlic
Italian herbs, to taste

2 dates, pitted and chopped
½ avocado
¼ red bell pepper
Olive oil for desired consistency
Salt, to taste
Pepper, to taste
Cayenne (optional)
½ cup sun-dried tomatoes
Onion, to taste
Chopped olives, to taste

Greens (Spinach)
3–4 cups spinach
Olive oil
Sea salt, to taste

Eggplant
Soak eggplant slices in salted water for 2–3 hours. Drain and spread on dehydrator trays and dehydrate for 30–45 minutes at 105°F.

Coating
In a food processor, blend all ingredients until almost smooth, but don't over process. Keep mixture thick.

Cheese
In a high-speed blender, combine all ingredients and blend until creamy.

Sauce
Combine sauce ingredients in a high-speed blender.

Greens (Spinach)

Clean and trim stems. Chop into smaller pieces. In a large bowl, drizzle a bit of olive oil and sea salt onto greens and massage with fingers to soften. Set aside.

Assembly

Lightly oil the bottom of a small glass baking dish. Arrange slices of eggplant in base of dish. Sprinkle and press on some coating mix to each slice with your fingers. Spread marinara sauce on top. Spread cheese mixture on top of sauce using an offset spatula. Add a light layer of spinach.

Continue layering in same order until all ingredients are used. Top with thin layer of cheese mixed with some of the under layer of marinara and don't go all the way to the edge, so that it looks like melted cheese on top when done.

Garnish top with a bit of chopped spinach and some of the coating mixture. Sprinkle with crushed red pepper and oregano. You could also use marinated and dehydrated mushroom slices and slivered olives to top off the dish as well. Or try adding a layer of Rawsages (page 111).

Dehydrate for several hours until eggplant is soft.

Pasta Primavera with Alfredo Sauce

Barbara Shevukun, Rawfully Tempting

Prep: 60 minutes

Alfredo Cream Sauce
1 cup cashews
½ cup macadamia nuts
½ water, or more to blend
2 cloves garlic, crushed
1 teaspoon miso
1 tablespoon olive oil
3 tablespoons onion
1 teaspoon raw honey or agave
Sea salt to taste

Marinade
2 tablespoons olive oil
½ teaspoon salt
Fresh basil, chopped
Italian herbs, to taste
Vegetables (such as carrots, Portobello mushrooms, onions,
    scallions, tomato, zucchini, baby eggplant, and yellow
    squash), sliced in thin strips and chopped

Parmesan Cheese
½ cup mixed almonds, pine nuts, and sesame seeds
Sea salt, to taste
Nutritional yeast (optional), to taste

Spaghetti Noodles
1 (12 oz.) package sea kelp noodles
Warm water
Lemon juice

Alfredo Cream Sauce
Mix ingredients in high-speed blender until creamy.

Marinade
Massage the first four ingredients into the assorted vegetables and let sit for 2 hours (or marinate for 1 hour and dehydrate for 1–2 hours at 110°F, placing in a glass bowl on bottom of your dehydrator).

Parmesan Cheese
Pulse process nuts and seeds in food processor. Add salt and nutritional yeast (optional). Mix.

Spaghetti Noodles
Rinse and soak kelp noodles in warm water with lemon juice for at last 30 minutes (the longer the better). Cut kelp noodles in half and mix with a bit of alfredo sauce. Massaging the cream into the noodles by hand is easier (and therapeutic).

You can top the creamy noodles with vegetables or you can mix some of the alfredo sauce into the vegetables first. You can also add a dollop of cream sauce to garnish the dish. It depends on how rich you like it.

Top with a sprinkle of Parmesan cheese and serve. Warm in dehydrator or lowest oven setting, if desired.

If you don't have kelp noodles readily available, you can spiralize zucchini for your pasta. Remember, the rule of thumb is to use one zucchini per person.

Vegetable Chili

Raw Chef Dan, Quintessence, New York, NY and Crucina, Madrid, Spain

Raw Chef Dan also teaches raw cooking classes and provides certification courses for raw chefs. His website is amazing. I've had the pleasure of taking many of his classes in person and on the web, and I always learn so much.

Prep: 20–30 minutes

3 cups water
2 cups tomatoes
1 red bell pepper
¼ cup sun-dried tomato
3 tablespoons onion, minced
2 tablespoons ginger, minced
2 tablespoons chili powder
1 teaspoon cumin
1 tablespoon oregano
2 cloves garlic
¼ cup cold-pressed olive oil
1 teaspoon sea salt

Blend in a high-speed blender until smooth. Serve with chunks of tomato slices, zucchini, and chopped red bell pepper.

Corny Sunshine Sandwich

Potlucker Linda Cooper, a. k. a. Linda Louise Cakes

Linda started out as a potlucker, and, as a result of her growing talent and exposure at potlucks, she has grown to be called "Linda Louise Cakes."

Corn Bread
Soak: 1–2 days
Dehydrate: 4–8 hours + 8 hours
Prep: 30–40 minutes

Deviled Egg Spread
Soak: 1–2 hours
Prep: 20 minutes

Corn Bread
1½ cups buckwheat groats, ground to flour, sprouted, and
    dehydrated
½ cup + ⅓ cup golden flax seeds, ground
½ cup sunflower seeds, sprouted, dehydrated, and ground
⅓ cup sunflower seed sprouts
⅓ cup pumpkin seeds, soaked
¼ cup sesame seeds
Kernels from 10 ears of corn
1 red pepper
½ yellow or orange pepper
1 teaspoon Celtic sea salt
1–2 teaspoons turmeric
Small quantity of fresh herbs of choice (I use dill)

Deviled Egg Spread
2 cups pine nuts, soaked 1–2 hours
½ cup sun-dried tomatoes, soaked 1–2 hours

1–2 tablespoons yellow miso
2 teaspoons cumin
2 teaspoons turmeric
Dash Celtic sea salt
¼ teaspoon fresh dill
2 sprigs fresh rosemary
2 basil leaves
¾ +/- cup water (just enough to blend)

Corn Bread
Place the groats and ½ cup of flax seeds, sunflower seeds, pumpkin seeds, and sesame seeds in a large bowl, and set aside. In a food processor, process the corn, red pepper, orange pepper, salt, turmeric, herbs, and ⅓ cup of flax seeds. Add the food processor contents to a bowl of mixed dry contents and stir well. Let rest for 1 hour or so, and then spread on oiled Teflex sheets and dry for about 8 hours. Flip and dry for about another 5 hours to desired texture (for the potluck, Linda hand-shaped the bread into sun shapes).

Deviled Egg Spread
Combine all the ingredients in a high-speed blender.

To Build Sandwich
Place the corn bread on the bottom, and top with Deviled Egg Spread, sliced grape tomatoes, and sprouts. Place the lid of the sandwich on top. You can add whatever ingredients that you like to your sandwich, like slices of pickles, onion rings, and lettuce. I also make the Deviled Egg Spread as a pâté and serve it with greens. One of the things that I love best about raw foods is you can mix and match. Use the Deviled Egg Spread from this recipe in another dish, such as Lasagna (see next page).

Lasagna La Zelinda

Linda Leboutillier, Waterloo Gardens

Linda started out as a potlucker, and now, will be adding a whole healthy division to her existing business of Waterloo Gardens (debuting in early 2010). Even if you do not live in the Philadelphia suburbs, Pennsylvania, or the United States, they will mail order to you. In fact, Linda is working on her own healthy cookbook. So, if you like this recipe, stay tuned: she will be creating many more.

Serves 8
Soak: 12 hours
Prep: 45–60 minutes
Dehydrate: warm in dehydrator 1–2 hours before serving (optional)

Artichoke Mixture
½ cup cold-pressed extra virgin olive oil
4 tablespoons fresh-squeezed lemon juice
1 teaspoon Himalayan sea salt
1 tablespoon Italian seasoning
½ teaspoon freshly ground pepper
⅛ teaspoon cayenne pepper
3 (12 oz.) packages frozen artichoke hearts, thawed and torn
        apart

Sunflower Seed Mixture
2 cups fresh basil
⅓ cup cold-pressed extra virgin olive oil
4 tablespoons fresh-squeezed lemon juice
1 teaspoon Himalayan salt
3 ½ cups sunflower seeds, soaked 12 hours, then drained
½ teaspoon freshly ground pepper
⅛ teaspoon cayenne pepper

Lasagna
6 large plum tomatoes, thinly sliced
¼ cup fresh basil leaves, minced
2 cups green olives, pitted
1 large red bell pepper, cleaned and diced

Artichoke Mixture
Mix together all the ingredients and marinate for 30 minutes.

Sunflower Seed Mixture
Mix together all the ingredients in a food processor until finely chopped.

Lasagna
Spray a 9- by 13-inch casserole dish with coconut or olive oil. Line the bottom of the casserole with the sunflower seed mixture, and then distribute the artichoke mixture evenly over the sunflower seed mixture.

Layer the tomatoes and basil over the artichoke mixture. Place the green olives and bell pepper in a food processor, pulse slightly, and then spread evenly over the tomato layer. Serve.

Nori Rolls with Sunflower Seed Filling

Brenda Cobb, Founder of Living Foods Institute® and author of The Living Foods Lifestyle *(www.livingfoodsinstitute.com), (800) 844-9876*

Prep: 30 minutes

Filling:
2 cups sunflower seeds
2 cloves garlic
⅔ cup fresh lemon juice
1 cup chopped green onions
¼ cup raw tahini
1 tablespoon powdered kelp seaweed
2 tablespoons dulse seaweed flakes
Pinch cayenne pepper

Nori Roll Assembly
Nori seaweed sheets (sun-dried raw sheets, not the toasted
        sheets)
Mixed baby greens
Red pepper strips, julienned
Carrot strips, julienned
Cucumber strips, julienned
Avocado, sliced
Sunflower or broccoli sprouts

Filling
Soak the sunflower seeds in filtered water for 4 hours and drain. In food processor chop the garlic into minced pieces and then add the sunflower seeds, lemon juice, green onions, raw tahini, kelp, dulse, and cayenne pepper. Process until smooth. You can put this in the fridge until you are ready to make the nori rolls. It will keep up to 3 days.

Nori Roll Assembly

Assemble nori rolls as close to serving time as possible because they tend to get soggy if they sit too long. Slice the avocado right before you are ready to make the rolls.

Place a nori sheet on your cutting board. Place a layer of mixed baby greens on the sheet, then spread 2 to 3 tablespoons of the sunflower seed filling on the greens. If you put the filling on top of the greens rather than next to the nori wrapper it will keep the wrapper from getting soggy.

Arrange the julienne vegetable strips on top of the filling and top with slices of avocado, then cover with sprouts. Carefully roll up the nori wrapper and seal using a little water on your fingertips. Slice into bite-sized pieces, rolls about 1-inch thick, and serve with wasabi and nama shoyu raw soy sauce.

Sweet and Spicy Thai Noodles

Karmyn Malone (www.Karmyn Malone.com)

Prep: 25 minutes
Serves: 2

Sauce
1 large, ripe mango, peeled and cubed
4 Roma tomatoes, quartered
½-inch ginger (more or less to taste)
1 Thai hot red pepper (more or less to taste)
1 medium sweet onion

Noodles
2 young Thai Coconuts

Assembly
4 Roma tomatoes
Scallions, to garnish

Sauce
Blend the ingredients together in a high-speed blender until smooth. If using a regular blender, a small of amount of water may be necessary.

Noodles
Open two young Thai coconuts, pour the coconut water into glasses (you can either serve this as your beverage or refrigerate for later use).

Scoop out the coconut meat and cut into noodles.

Assembly
Layer the noodles into two bowls.

Add a layer of two chopped Roma tomatoes into each bowl.

Pour equal amounts of prepared sauce in each bowl. Chop a scallion or two and sprinkle on top of the sauce (can substitute any herb or green . . . this step gives the dish color).

Enjoy!

Unmacaroni Salad

Lisa Montgomery

16 ounces mushrooms, sliced
1 head cauliflower, chopped into bite-sized pieces
1½ cups Raw Mayonnaise (see page 130)
3 tablespoons lemon juice
½ teaspoon celery seed
2 cups celery, chopped
1 small jar pimento, finely chopped
1 red pepper, finely chopped
Sea salt to taste
Agave to taste

Combine the ingredients in a large mixing bowl, making sure that the Raw Mayonnaise thoroughly coats all of the ingredients. You can either eat as is or serve on a bed of greens.

Raw Mayonnaise

Janice Innella, The Beauty Chef

Prep: 10 minutes

1 cup raw cashews
2 young Thai coconuts, meat only
1 lemon, juiced
1 teaspoon raw honey
1 teaspoon sea salt
½ cup raw olive oil, cold-pressed
⅛ teaspoon cayenne

In a blender, add all the ingredients and blend until smooth. Chill.

Un-"Meatloaf"

Joel Odhner, Catalyst Cleanse, Rawlife Line, Philadelphia, PA

"Meatloaf"
Soak: nuts and seeds, 4–5 hours
Prep: 30 minutes
Dehydrate: 1 + 2–3 hours at 115°F

Barbeque Sauce
Prep: 10 minutes

"Meatloaf"
¾ cup walnuts
1 cup sunflower seeds
1 cup almonds
Filtered water, for soaking seeds and almonds
2 cloves garlic
½ cup parsley, chopped
½ cup celery, chopped
1 cup red bell pepper, chopped
1 cup portabella mushroom, marinated (optional)
1 tablespoon onion, chopped
2 tablespoons rosemary
1 tablespoon tarragon
1 tablespoon jalapeño
1 teaspoon cumin

Barbeque Sauce
1 cup tomatoes
½ cup sun-dried tomatoes
¼ cup onion, chopped
1 clove garlic

½ teaspoon jalapeño or chili powder
4 fresh basil leaves
¼ cup Braggs or sea salt
¼ cup cold-pressed olive oil

"Meatloaf"
Homogenize seeds, nuts, and garlic in a food processor. Pour the homogenized seeds, nuts, and garlic in a large mixing bowl. Stir the remaining ingredients with the nuts, seeds, and garlic mixture. Form into a loaf. Dehydrate for 1 hour.

Barbeque Sauce
Blend together in a high-speed blender and spoon over the "meatloaf" after it has dehydrated for 1 hour. Then put the "meatloaf" back in the dehydrator for another 2–3 hours.

Nori Rolls

Joel Odhner, Catalyst Cleanse, Rawlife Line, Philadelphia, PA

Prep: 30 minutes

Rice

4 cups jicama, chopped

½ cup cashews or pine nuts

¼ cup rice wine vinegar or apple cider vinegar

3 tablespoons agave nectar

Filling

4–6 sheets raw nori

1 red pepper, julienned

3 celery ribs, julienned

1 zucchini, julienned

4–6 marinated shitake mushrooms (optional)

1 avocado, sliced (optional)

Handful of your favorite sprouts

Rice

Place jicama and nuts in a food processor, and process until rice-sized. Place the mixture in a nut milk bag and squeeze the moisture out. Place in a bowl and mix in the remaining ingredients.

Filling

Lay out nori sheets on a clean, dry surface. Place ½ cup of rice on nori and spread evenly over the bottom third of the sheet. Place vegetables on the rice. Carefully roll the nori. Wet the top edge of the nori with a little water to seal. Let the nori roll stand for 5 minutes. Cut with a sharp knife.

Enjoy plain, or you can use Braggs, chopped ginger, or agave mixture.

Pad Thai

Joel Odhner, Catalyst Cleanse, Rawlife Line, Philadelphia, PA

Prep: 30 minutes

Noodles
Green and red cabbage, julienned
Zucchini, julienned
Young Thai coconut meat, julienned
Red and yellow peppers, julienned

Sauce
1 cup young Thai coconut meat
½ cup young Thai coconut water
½ cup macadamia or Brazil nuts
1 clove garlic
⅛ cup lime or lemon juice
½ teaspoon sea salt
½ teaspoon ginger chopped
Pinch of cayenne

Noodles
Combine all the ingredients and set aside.

Sauce
Place all the ingredients in a high-speed blender, and blend until smooth. Mix the sauce with the noodles, and let stand for 30 minutes. Lasts for 2 days in the refrigerator.

Portobello Mock Meatloaf

Sheryl Chavarria, Raw Can Roll Café, Pure Body Spa, Douglasville, PA

Soak: 2–4 hours
Prep: 20–30 minutes
Dehydrate: 1–2 hours at 115°F

Meatloaf
2½ cups sunflower seeds, soaked
2 cups walnuts, soaked
3 cups portobello mushrooms
1 cup yellow or red bell pepper
½ cup onion
½ cup parsley (can substitute rosemary or use ¼ cup parsley
        and ¼ cup rosemary)
2–3 cloves garlic, pressed
1 cup celery
1 tablespoon cumin
¼ cup wheat-free tamari
½ cup olive oil

Tomato Paste Sauce
1 cup tomato
¼ cup fresh basil
2 sun-dried tomatoes
1 tablespoon agave or raw honey
Salt to taste

Meatloaf
Place soaked nuts, seeds, and mushrooms into a food processor, and process until smooth. Add the rest of the ingredients to the food processor, and process to desired "meatloaf" consistency.

Form into a meatloaf shape and dehydrate for 1–2 hours at 115°F, cut into thin slices, and serve. Can also top with a tomato-paste sauce.

Tomato Paste Sauce
Combine the ingredients in a high-speed blender until well-blended. Paint the top of the mock meatloaf.

Sea Spaghetti Alfredo

Tiffany Watts, Oasis Living Cuisine, Frazer, PA (www. oasislivingcuisine.com)

Tiffany brought this "Main Event" dish to a raw potluck, and it was one of the hits of the dinner.

Sea Spaghetti
Soak: sea spaghetti, 30 minutes
Prep: 20 minutes

Alfredo Sauce
Soak: sun-dried tomatoes, 15 minutes
Prep: 15 minutes

Sea Spaghetti
2 bags sea spaghetti, soaked, drained, and rinsed
1 cup carrots, shredded
1 cup zucchini, shredded

Alfredo Sauce
2 cups spring water
¾ cup cashews
½ cup macadamia nuts
5 sun-dried tomatoes
½ teaspoon onion powder
½ clove garlic
½ teaspoon salt
⅛ teaspoon cayenne pepper

Sea Spaghetti
Soak sea spaghetti for 30 minutes, rinse, and drain.

Alfredo Sauce
Blend all the ingredients for the alfredo sauce in a high-speed blender until smooth.
Toss the alfredo sauce with sea spaghetti and vegetables.

Raw Baby Food

Jinje's (The GardenDiet.com) seven-year-old daughter Shale came up with this recipe for her one-year old sister Yarrow to eat. It is a delicious green baby food that has purslane in it, which is a green herb that has both a wonderful sour flavor that kids love, and an awesome essential fatty acid content that their growing brains need.

Prep: 15 minutes

½ bunch purslane

1 pear

A few peas, leaves of basil, and sprig of dill (or alternate a few pinches of whatever other yummy greens or veggies that you might have around)

Blend all of the above in a high-speed blender until baby-food consistency.

Yarrow could not get enough of this lovely dark-green and tasty treat, which any baby should love.

So, if little Shale can be creative in creating raw food from her garden, so can you.

Chinese Veggie Stir-Fry Surprise

Barbara Shevkun, Rawfully Tempting

Prep: 30 minutes

Marinade
2 tablespoons olive oil
1 tablespoon coconut water vinegar
1 tablespoon nama shoyu
1–2 teaspoons sesame oil
1 teaspoon ginger
1 clove garlic, crushed
1 teaspoon lemon juice

Noodles
Zucchini
Kelp noodles (or bean thread noodles soaked in hot water—not
    raw, but really yummy)

Veggies
Carrots, zucchini, bok choy, broccoli, Chinese cabbage, shitake
    mushrooms, mushrooms, bell peppers, fresh baby corn,
    red onions, snow peas or any other delicious veggies

Marinade
Blend the ingredients together in a high-speed blender. Adjust to
taste.

Noodles
Spiralize the zucchini and mix with the kelp noodles. Set aside.

Veggies
Marinate veggies in marinade for two hours, stirring occasionally.
Dehydrate 1–2 hours. Stir and serve over noodles, then garnish
with sesame seeds or slivered almonds.

Hot & Spicy

Alorah Arliotis (www.thewiserwoman.co.uk), Glastonbury, England

Prep: 20 minutes

1 cup walnuts, soaked
1 cup carrots, chopped
1 cup celery, chopped
3–4 sun-dried tomatoes, soaked
Pinch sea salt
½ teaspoon cumin powder
½ teaspoon turmeric powder
½ teaspoon paprika
A splash extra virgin olive oil
1 orange, juiced
1 teaspoon agave
½ cup coriander or cilantro, chopped

Place ingredients in a high-speed blender or food processor and process until mixture forms a pâté consistency. If too thick, add a little water, making sure to add very slowly to ensure pâté consistency. Pâté can be used to top your salad as a Main Event, as a filling for a wrap, or on raw crackers.

Romaine Almond Crackers

Alorah Arliotis (www.thewiserwoman.co.uk), Glastonbury England

Prep: 25 minutes

1 head romaine lettuce
1 cup almond pulp
1 to 1½ cups ground flax seeds
1 teaspoon Italian herbs
1 teaspoon kelp flakes
¼ teaspoon cayenne pepper
½ cup flax seed oil
½ cup water
Sea salt to taste

Chop lettuce in a food processor very quickly. Do not let it get mushy. Combine all ingredients to form a sticky dough. Roll out on a baking sheet lined with baking parchment. Dehydrate for 6–7 hours. Cool. Store in an air-tight container.

Dandelion Pesto

Sergei Boutenko, The Raw Family, author of many books such as
Ultimate Live Food Cookbook *and DVD* The Miracle of Greens.

To find out how to get fresh dandelions, go to Boutenko's website and watch Sergei's videos. Sergei is an expert in incorporating wild edibles into your diet. So, you do not even have to plant a "raw garden" for many of Sergei's recipes. You can just go and forage on your own back-yard, or go for a walk in the meadow, climb a mountain, or stroll by a river. Mother Nature provides the gardening for you.

Serves 3
Prep: 20 minutes

3 ½ cups dandelion leaves and flowers
½ cup sunflower seeds
2–3 cloves garlic
¼ cup basil greens, fresh or dried
1 tablespoon cold-pressed olive oil
1 tablespoon lemon juice
1 teaspoon sea salt (optional)
¼ cup sun-dried tomatoes (optional)

Place all the ingredients in a blender, and blend thoroughly. Add more oil or lemon juice, if necessary. Serve as you would regular pesto (for example, on crackers, bread, or pasta). Decorate with dandelion flowers.

Roasted Bell Pepper Cheese & Mushroom Risotto

Raw Chef Dan, Quintessence, New York, NY

Prep: 30 minutes

2 whole red or yellow bell peppers
¼ cup cold-pressed olive oil from a dark bottle
4 teaspoons sea salt
2–3 dried chipotle peppers (for less heat, remove seeds)
1 cup pine nuts
1 cup macadamia nuts
3½–4 cups yellow squash (finished quantity), chopped to rice consistency
2 cups button or cremini mushrooms, sliced
Parsley for garnish

Blend the bell peppers, olive oil, sea salt, and chipotles in a high-speed blender. I tend to use less than 1 dried chipotle pepper, because my body cannot handle that much heat. You may want to start with just a ½ of a chipotle, and then add another ½, blend, and keep taste-testing just to make sure that it is the right heat for you.

Add pine and macadamia nuts to the mixture. Blend to a thick cream and set aside.

Put chopped yellow squash in the food processor with the S-blade, and pulse chop until you get a rice-like consistency. Process until you get about 3½-4 cups.

Transfer all the ingredients to a mixing bowl, and add 2 cups of sliced button or cramini mushrooms and mix together. Garnish with chopped parsley when serving.

Spring Roll

Joel Odhner, Catalyst Cleanse, Rawlife Line, Philadelphia, PA

Prep: 30 minutes

Filling
Soak: nuts, 2–4 hours

Wrap
1 head Napa cabbage

Filling
1 cup Brazil nuts, soaked
1 cup walnuts, soaked
¼ teaspoon sea salt
½ tablespoon sage
⅛ cup lemon juice
½ cup olive oil
½ clove garlic
½ cup cilantro, chopped

Spicy Mustard
½ cup mustard seed, soaked, with soaking water
⅛ cup lemon juice
½ cup agave nectar
¼ teaspoon sea salt

Filling
Place all the ingredients (except the cilantro) in a food processor and blend until smooth. Gently mix in the cilantro.

Spicy Mustard
Place the mustard ingredients in a high-powered blender, and blend until smooth.

Place ¼–½ cup of filling on a Napa cabbage leaf and drizzle with spicy mustard. Roll up and enjoy. Lasts 3–5 days refrigerated.

This is another great dish to pack in your lunch each day.

Summer Wrap

Joel Odhner, Catalyst Cleanse, Rawlife Line, Philadelphia, PA

Prep: 30 minutes

Wrap
1 large collard leaf
½ avocado, diced
1 plum tomato, diced
¼ cup Vidalia onion, diced

Honey Mustard
¼ cup cold-pressed olive oil
¼ cup fresh lemon juice
¼ cup apple cider vinegar (optional)
1 tablespoon ground mustard
1 clove garlic, minced
2 teaspoons agave nectar
½ teaspoon cumin
Pinch sea salt

Wrap
Combine avocado, plum tomato, and Vidalia onion. Place the mixture in collard leaf, drizzle with Honey Mustard, and add sea salt and pepper to taste. Fold top and stem ends of the collard leaf in, and roll up burrito style.

Honey Mustard
Blend all the ingredients in a high-powered blender. Add water to reach desired consistency.

Tabouli

Joel Odhner, Catalyst Cleanse, Rawlife Line, Philadelphia, PA

Prep: 20 minutes

4 cups parsley, finely chopped
2 large broccoli stems, chopped
2 cups tomatoes, diced
½ cup lemon juice
¼ cup cold-pressed olive oil
2 cucumbers, finely chopped
½ bunch mint, finely chopped
Sea salt and pepper to taste

Chop broccoli stems in a food processor into bite-sized pieces. Place broccoli in a bowl and add the remaining ingredients. Toss and serve.

Turkey Nut Burgers

Janice Innella, The Beauty Chef

Soak: nuts, 1 hour
Dehydrate: 4 hours
Prep: 30–40 minutes

1 cup pecans

1 cup walnuts

1 cup pine nuts

3 tablespoons cold-pressed olive oil

1 medium zucchini

½ cup Austria's Finest, Naturally pumpkin seeds, ground

1 bunch fresh basil

1 tablespoon sage

1-inch sprig of rosemary

⅛ teaspoon cayenne pepper

1 teaspoon Celtic sea salt

1 teaspoon thyme

1 rib celery, finely chopped

Soak nuts for 1 hour; drain well. Hand-chop your celery and set aside. Process the remaining ingredients in your food processor. Combine the hand-chopped celery with the mixture, mold into medium-size burgers, and dehydrate for 4 hours.

Serve the Turkey Nut Burgers with Mashed Taters and Miso Gravy (see pages 92 and 93).

Veggie Medley

Joel Odhner, Catalyst Cleanse, Rawlife Line, Philadelphia, PA

Prep: 20–30 minutes
Stand: 30 minutes

½ pound asparagus, chopped into 1-inch pieces
1 cup tomatoes, diced
1 red or yellow pepper, diced
½ cup broccoli florets, chopped
¼ cup basil, julienned
¼ cup parsley, chopped
⅛ cup cold-pressed olive oil
⅛ cup lemon juice
Sea salt to taste

Combine all the ingredients in a bowl and let stand for 30 minutes.
Lasts 2–3 days refrigerated.

Nori Rolls
Lisa Montgomery

When I make this, I tend to store the filling in a sealed plastic container. I also store the sliced vegetables in another plastic container so that way if I am packing this for lunch several days in a row, I just build my nori rolls each day to save time and to keep them fresher when I don't have the luxury of making the dish right before I eat it.

Prep: 30 minutes

Filling
3 tablespoons white miso
¼–½ teaspoon toasted sesame oil

Assembly
Raw nori sheets
Assorted vegetables, thinly sliced

Filling
Combine the miso and toasted sesame oil and set aside. This keeps in a sealed container for a week.

Assembly
Spread the filling on a raw nori sheet which you lay out (shiny side down) on a bamboo sushi mat. Spread the miso filling over the first inch of the nori sheet. Then fill with your favorite vegetables (such as carrots, celery, cucumber, mushrooms, onion, sprouts, red pepper, and avocados). Lay the thinly sliced vegetables across the nori sheet then roll up starting with the end closest to you. Seal the end of the nori roll with water. Cut the long nori roll into 1-inch pieces.

    I use wheat-free tamari as a dipping sauce.

Sweet Vegetable Marinade

Lisa Montgomery

Prep: 30 minutes

Marinade
½ cup orange juice, freshly squeezed
1 tablespoon agave
1 tablespoon cold-cold pressed olive oil
Sea salt to taste

Vegetables
Assorted vegetables, sliced into bite-sized pieces

Marinade
Combine ingredients in a high-speed blender and set aside.

Vegetables
Toss the vegetables into the marinade. You can even add dried cranberries and pineapples to add pop as well. Place marinated vegetables in a glass dish and place in Tribest Sedona Dehydrator at 105°F for 1 hour. This dish tastes great warm as well as chilled. You can serve this as a stand-alone dish, on greens, or as a side dish.

Asian Vegetable Medley

Lisa Montgomery

Prep: 30 minutes

Marinade
½ cup wheat-free tamari
1 teaspoon toasted sesame oil
1 tablespoon cold-pressed olive oil
1 tablespoon olive oil
1 clove garlic, minced
Pinch sea salt
¼–½ teaspoon grated ginger

Vegetables
Assorted Asian vegetables (such as shitake mushrooms, snow
       peas, mung bean sprouts, Asian cabbage or bok choy,
       scallions, cauliflower florets, and jicama)

Marinade
Combine the ingredients in a high-speed blender and set aside.

Vegetables
Slice and chop the vegetables into bite-sized pieces. If using jicama, you can peel and grate it for a rice-like effect.

Combine vegetables with marinade, making sure the vegetables are totally coated. Transfer coated vegetables to a glass dish and place in Tribest Sedona Dehydrator for 1 hour at 105°F. You can also add pieces of raw cashews to add a little more Asian flair.

Pickles (Bubbie's Raw Pickles)

Lisa Montgomery

Prep: 10 minutes
Dehydrate: Overnight

Bubbie's pickles (dill chips or spears)
Nutritional Yeast Flakes
Assorted dried seasonings

I just took the dill chips as well as the spears (sliced), rolled them in the Nutritional Yeast Flakes, and dehydrated them until reaching the desired consistency. If you want assorted flavors, you can roll in sea salt, Italian seasoning, cajun seasoning, or pizza seasoning. Whatever works for you!

I threw the left-over Nutritional Yeast Flakes out for my chickens, and they loved it. They looked so cute with yellow Nutritional Yeast Flakes on their beaks. I know, only faces that a mother could love.

You can also make your own pickles using the Perfect Pickler (perfectpickler.com). I did this last summer, using heirloom-organic cucumbers that I grew in my own raised-bed garden. It is so cool growing the cucumbers, pickling them, and then eating them, especially in the winter time.

Cheesy Kale Chips

Lisa Montgomery

In Raw Inspiration: Living Dynamically With Raw Foods, *I shared how to make your basic kale chips. This recipe takes it one step farther, and I must confess that it is to die for. I also use the "Cheese" recipe as a dip and dressing.*

Prep: 20 minutes
Dehydrate: Overnight or 4–8 hours at 105°F

Cheese
⅔ cup cashews
4 tablespoons lemon juice
1 tablespoon agave
6 tablespoons water
½ cup cold-pressed olive oil
1½ teaspoons sea salt
½ cup nutritional yeast
1 teaspoon turmeric
5 cloves garlic, minced
⅛ cup red onion, chopped
Dash Herbamare

Kale Chips
2–4 bunches kale

Cheese
Combine the ingredients in a high-speed blender until creamy and smooth. Add more or less water for desired consistency. I tend to double the recipe so I have plenty to coat my kale, and then keep the rest as a dressing.

Kale Chips

Rip kale off of stems, and place in a bowl. Pour the Cheese over the kale, and, with your hands, make sure that the kale is totally covered. Place on Teflex-coated sheets, and then place in your dehydrator. Dehydrate overnight, and, by the time that you wake up the next morning, they are ready for you to eat. If you make them during the day, one tends to walk by the dehydrator, eating them in the process, and they are good that way, as well.

For basic kale chips, place de-stemmed shredded kale in a mixing bowl, sprinkle sea salt to flavor, and add enough Austria's Finest, Naturally pumpkin seed oil or cold-pressed olive oil to cover the kale. Place on Teflex sheets on trays in a dehydrator for approximately 4–6 hours at 105°F.

Raw Prepared Mustard

Rhio, Hooked on Raw

This is a good substitute for cooked Dijon mustard.

Prep: 10 minutes

7 tablespoons whole brown mustard seeds
1½ tablespoon whole yellow mustard seeds
3 tablespoons raw apple cider vinegar
3 ounces filtered water
1½ tablespoons raw unheated honey
½ teaspoon Celtic sea salt

In a pint glass jar combine the whole mustard seeds, apple cider vinegar, and water and give the mixture a gentle stir.

Cap the jar, but not tightly, and let sit at room temperature for 24 hours.

After 24 hours, put the mixture into a blender, add the honey and Celtic sea salt, then blend well. You will have to stop the machine and push the mustard down a few times. You might also have to add a little more filtered water, but do this one tablespoon at a time until it becomes a mustard consistency.

Store in a glass jar in the refrigerator. Makes 1 cup. Keeps for months.

If you close the jar too tightly, some pressure might build up in the jar... mustard is potent.

The first time you make this recipe, try making it as stated above to see if it suits you. To make a hotter mustard, simply increase the ratio of yellow mustard seeds. To make a milder mustard, increase the brown mustard seeds and decrease the yellow.

To make a simple salad dressing, add ½ teaspoon of Raw Prepared Mustard to olive and flaxseed oils, fresh lemon juice, fresh prepared garlic, and Celtic sea salt. I also use this as a condiment with raw veggie burgers. Use it anywhere you would use Dijon mustard.

BBQ Sauce

Linda Cooper (a. k. a. Linda Louise Cakes)

This BBQ Sauce is good on kale chips, but also as a dip or dressing. Great over enoki mushrooms to act as a pulled pork or spaghetti sauce over spiralized zucchini.

Prep: 20 minutes
Soak: sun-dried tomatoes and raisins, 30 minutes

1–2 cups tomatoes, chopped
½ cup sun-dried tomatoes, soaked for 30 minutes, and drained
¼–½ cup raisins, soaked for 30 minutes, and drained
1 slice red onion
½ teaspoon cumin
1 lemon, juiced
½ avocado

Soak the sun-dried tomatoes and raisins for 30 minutes. Drain, saving the soaking water in case you need it to thin the recipe. Blend all the ingredients together until well-blended, adding the avocado in last.

Mushroom Cake

Raw Chef Dan, Quintessence, New York, NY and Crucina, Madrid, Spain

Prep: 25 minutes

2 tablespoons raw soy sauce
¼ cup water
1 tablespoon garlic, minced
1 tablespoon sage, chopped
1 tablespoon oregano, chopped
1 tablespoon dill, chopped
½ cup scallions, chopped
1 cup shredded trumpet or canary mushrooms
¼ cup ground golden flax seed

In a small mixing bowl combine raw soy sauce, water, and garlic. Then add the sage, oregano, dill, scallion, and shredded mushrooms. Slowly add in the flax powder as you mix the ingredients together until it thickens and starts to cling. Let set about 15 minutes until the ingredients stick together.

Form into small medallions using about two tablespoons per each mushroom cake. Place on a teflex sheet and dehydrate at 100°F for 2 hours then flip, removing the teflex and continue to dehydrate another 3 hours.

Note: If you can't find trumpet or canary mushrooms, you can use the top 1½ inch of a portobello stem. They can all be peeled or shredded like crab meat.

JayBee's Café Sun Burger

Jacquelyne Rennie, JayBee's Café, Skippack, PA (www.jaybeescafe.com)

Prep: 25 minutes

1 cup walnuts, soaked for 2 hours
1 cup pumpkin seeds, soaked for 4 hours
8 medium-sized sun-dried tomatoes, halved, soaked for 4 hours
    (reserve the liquid)
½ cup mushroom stems
2 tablespoons Bragg's Liquid Amino
½ cup carrots, shredded
1 teaspoon chili powder
1 teaspoon fresh basil
½ teaspoon fresh garlic, minced
3 tablespoons olive oil

Rinse and drain the nuts and seeds. Drain the sun-dried tomatoes and reserve the juices. Place all of the ingredients in blender on low speed. Add the sun-dried tomato liquid and puree.

Using a ½ cup dry measuring cup, form the ingredients into patties. Place on teflex sheet and dehydrate at 105°F for 4 hours. Take out of the dehydrator and they are ready to serve.

Jackie places these on a nice green salad and her customers love them!

Squash Pâté /Dip

Potlucker Sue Roseman

In memory of Potlucker Sue Roseman

Prep: 25 minutes

¼ cup sunflower seeds

2 tablespoons walnuts

1½ cups grated butternut squash (you can do this yourself, or
buy it already chunked, and then grate it in the food
processor)

Nuts

½ avocado

1 tablespoon Braggs

¼ cup sweet onion, chopped

Squash (see above)

1 tablespoon lemon juice

¼ cup celery, chopped

½ cup sun-dried tomatoes, soaked and drained (can add more
sun-dried tomatoes for extra flavor)

Soak the sun-dried tomatoes for 30 minutes.

Grind the walnuts and sunflower seeds in a food processor and
set aside.

In a high-speed blender on the lowest speed, use the tapper to
blend all the ingredients thoroughly.

Fruit & Nut Crackers

Potlucker Tess Jenson, Kaleidoscope Angels

Prep: 30 minutes
Sit: 20 minutes
Dehydrate: 115°F for 6 hours + 8 hours

¾ cup pineapple chunks
1 tart apple, cored
½ cup raisins, craisins, or any dried fruit of choice
1 cup flax seed, roughly ground
1 cup carrot pulp
1 cup carrot juice
½ cup pecan, walnuts, or almonds
¾ teaspoon cinnamon
½ teaspoon nutmeg
½ teaspoon ginger
¼ teaspoon salt

Combine pineapple, apple, nuts, and dried fruit in the food processor, using the S-blade, and pulsing until finely chopped (not pureed). Add chopped flax seed, carrot pulp, carrot juice, and spices. Stir well until well-blended. Let sit for 20 minutes, and then spread on Teflex sheets and dehydrate at 115°F for 6 hours. Cut into desired shapes. Continue dehydrating for 8 more hours. This is a very flexible recipe: you can add whatever you enjoy.

Carrot-Ginger Dip

Potlucker Tess Jenson, Kaleidoscope Angels

Prep: 25 minutes

5 large carrots, chopped
⅓ cup cold-pressed extra virgin olive oil
¼ cup raw tahini
3 tablespoons nama shoyu
3 tablespoons apple cider vinegar
3 tablespoons fresh ginger, peeled and chopped
2 tablespoons raw honey
1 clove garlic
½ teaspoon anise seed or licorice root
Pinch cinnamon, curry, cardamom, turmeric, cumin, and
    cayenne

Blend all the ingredients in a blender until smooth.

Sweet-Meets-Heat Seed Sandwich

Potlucker Linda Cooper (a. k. a. Linda Louise Cakes)

Prep: 30 minutes
Dehydrate: 110°F for 24 +/- hours

2 apples, cored
2 pears, cored
Juice of 1 lemon
2 tablespoons raw honey
½ cup raisins, soaked for ½ hour +/-
1 teaspoon cinnamon
¼-½ cup almond flour

Make a bath of Janice Innella's Pumpkin Spice Beauty Snack (see page 164). Dry both sides and leave uncut on a mesh screen.

Blend the ingredients to puree in a high-speed blender. Can use raisin-soak water, if needed, to get the blender turning.

Spread a generous layer of fruit filling on the pumpkin cracker. Sprinkle raisins on top of the puree, and press down to embed into the puree. Dehydrate 24 hours or until dry. Make another batch of Pumpkin Spice Beauty Snack, and spread an even layer on top of the dried fruit filling. Dehydrate another 24 hours or more until dry. Cut into desired shapes and enjoy. This will make more crackers than you have fruit filling, so enjoy the extra crackers, or make extra filling to cover the crackers.

Pumpkin Spice Beauty Snack

Janice Innella, The Beauty Chef

Soak: pumpkin seeds; 8 hours
Sprout: pumpkin seeds; 4 hours or less
Soak: flax seeds; 4 hours
Prep: 70 minutes (including waiting time)
Dehydrate: 18 hours at 115°F

2 cups pumpkin seeds, soaked and sprouted
1 cup golden flaxseed, soaked in 2 cups water
1 cup pumpkin seeds, ground
1 cup golden flaxseed, ground
2 cups pure water
2 lemons, juiced
2 tablespoons lemon zest
1 teaspoon cayenne pepper
1 tablespoon Celtic sea salt or ½ tablespoon Himalayan pink
    sea salt
4 tablespoons olive oil, hemp seed oil, or Austria's Finest,
    Naturally pumpkin seed oil
1 large red onion, minced finely
1 tablespoon caraway seed, ground

Soak pumpkin seeds for 8 hours, and then rinse and sprout for 4 hours. Soak flax seeds in 2 cups of water and let sit for 4 hours. In a large bowl, mix by hand all the ingredients thoroughly. Let sit for 20 minutes. Then use a spatula to evenly spread the mixture onto about 5 Teflex sheets. Score into small 1-inch crackers or larger, if desired. Set a dehydrator to 115°F and dry for 12 hours. Flip the trays with another tray on top, and then peel off the Teflex sheet and dehydrate for another 6 hours. Store in a cool, dry container.

This recipe is a low-carb, low-calorie snack, especially good for those with diabetes. Beautifying effects are from the rich omegas in the pumpkin seeds and the high fiber in the flaxseed: beauty from the inside out.

Veggie Dill Crackers

Janice Innella, The Beauty Chef

Prep: 25 minutes
Dehydrate: 12 + 12 hours
Sprout: 1–2 days

3 cups sunflower seeds, sprouted
2 cups golden flax seeds (1 cup will be ground in a coffee
      grinder)
4 cups water
2 red peppers, seeded and chopped
½ cup fresh dill
1 teaspoon Celtic sea salt or more, if you like
1 chili pepper
2 shallots or ½ red onion (medium-size)
3 tablespoons cold-pressed olive oil

Grind all the ingredients in a food processor and spread on Teflex
sheets. Pre-score crackers with a knife. Dehydrate for 12 hours,
flip, and dry for another 12 hours at 105°F.

Austria's Finest, Naturally Trail Mix

Austria's Finest, Naturally, Helco Ltd., Mt. Vernon, VA (www. austrianpumpkinoil.com)

Prep: 15 minutes

2 cups Austria's Finest, Naturally pumpkin seeds
½ cup sunflower seeds
½ cup dried blueberries, cranberries, or black currants
Pecans or walnuts

Mix together and enjoy.

Creamy Spinach Dip

Elaina Love, Pure Joy Planet, author of Elaina Love's Pure Joy Kitchen,
Volumes 1 and 2

Prep: 25 minutes
Serves 8

2 zucchinis, chopped
¼ cup water
1½ cups cashews
⅓ cup light miso
1 teaspoon Himalayan crystal salt
1 tablespoon lemon juice
1 tablespoon onion powder
3 cloves garlic
½ teaspoon white pepper
¼ teaspoon nutmeg
Pinch of cayenne
2–3 heads of spinach (about 10 cups)

Place the zucchini and water in a blender, and blend until smooth. Add the remainder of the ingredients (except the spinach). Blend until creamy. You may need to use a spatula or celery stick to get the mixture to blend. Pulse the spinach in a food processor until it is well-chopped. Mix all the prepared ingredients together in a bowl. This dish will keep 3 or more days in the refrigerator.

I prefer South River miso, as it is gluten-free.

Curry Dill Pâté

Joel Odhner, Catalyst Cleanse, Rawlife Line, Philadelphia, PA

Prep: 20 minutes
Soak: nuts; 2–4 hours

2 cups pecans, soaked
2 cups cauliflower, chopped
1 tablespoon curry powder
1 tablespoon dill weed
1 tablespoon cold-pressed extra virgin olive oil
1 tablespoon lemon juice
1 teaspoon Celtic sea salt

Combine all of the ingredients in a food processor until smooth.

Delicious Spinach Chips

Victoria Boutenko (rawfamily.com), author and creator of the "Green Smoothie." Victoria's Green Smoothie has gone around the world—even Harvard now recognizes its health benefits. I like it for the taste. Thank you, Victoria.

Prep: 10 minutes
Dehydrate: 105°F until crunchy

1 pound fresh spinach greens
1 lemon, juiced

Place spinach leaves on dehydrator sheets and sprinkle with lemon juice. Dehydrate at 105°F until crunchy.

Annie's Guacamole

Annie Marshall, Fante's Kitchen Ware Shop, Philadelphia, PA

Prep: 20 minutes

3 ripe avocados
¼-½ cup onion (approximately), chopped
1 clove garlic, chopped
½ lime, juiced
10 springs fresh cilantro, chopped
1 fresh whole tomato, chopped
1 jalapeño pepper, chopped (seeded if you do not want it to be
    too hot)
Salt and pepper to taste

Mix all of the ingredients together in a bowl, but not too much. The guacamole is meant to be lumpy. To store, place plastic wrap directly on top of the mix to keep the guacamole from oxidizing and turning brown. I have read that keeping 1 of the pits from the avocado in the dip will also help to keep it from turning brown.

Cashew Cheeseless Spread

Bruce and Marsha Weinstein, Awesome Foods, Bridgeport, PA
(www.awesomefoods.com)

Prep: 30 minutes

15 ounces Cashew Cream (10 ounces cashews, 5 ounces water)
4½ ounces yellow pepper
2½ ounces fresh lemon juice
2 teaspoons dried parsley
1½ tablespoons dried dill
1⅔ teaspoons dried basil
1 teaspoon black pepper
1 teaspoon granulated garlic
1 teaspoon granulated onion
½ teaspoon sesame seeds
⅙ teaspoon Himalayan sea salt

Grind cashews in a food processor, and then add water and process to make the cream. Add the rest of the ingredients until smooth.

In addition to being used as a cheese spread, you can dehydrate it, and turn it into crackers or cashew-dill cheese sticks.

All ounces are measured by weight. They are not to be measured in a measuring cup.

Tostadas or Corn Chips
Frederic Patenaude's New Year's Day Menu
(www.fredericpatenaude.com)

Prep: 20 minutes
Makes 2 dehydrator trays of chips or 6 tostada shells

Tostadas
Dehydrate: 105°F for 8–12 hours + 8–12 hours

Corn Chips
Dehydrate: 105°F for 2 hours + 12 hours + 12–18 hours

4 cups fresh corn kernels
½ cup purified water
1 teaspoon Celtic sea salt
¼ cup golden flax seeds, ground
¼ cup hemp seeds

Blend corn, water, and salt in a high-speed blender on high until smooth. Add hemp seeds and ground flax seeds, and then blend on low speed until mixed together, leaving the seeds whole.

Tostadas
On a dehydrator mesh tray, place a Teflex sheet. Measure ⅓ cup of the mixture and place in each of the four corners on top of the Teflex sheet. Using a spoon, smooth out the mixture in a round form with a diameter of 6 inches or 15 centimeters. Dehydrate at 105°F for 8–12 hours. Remove the Teflex sheet by flipping the sheet over onto the mesh dehydrator tray. Gently peel off the Teflex sheet by lifting 1 corner of the sheet and pulling it off until completely removed. Place the tray in the dehydrator and dehydrate at 105°F for 12–18 hours until shells are crispy. Let them cool. Store in a

sealed container in a cool, dark place, preferably in a refrigerator or freezer.

Corn Chips

On a dehydrator mesh tray, place a Teflex sheet. Spread half of the mixture on top of each Teflex sheet. Dehydrate at 105°F for 2 hours. Score the mixture into 64 triangles. Dehydrate further at 105°F for 12 hours. Remove the Teflex sheet by flipping the sheet over onto the mesh dehydrator tray. Gently peel off the Teflex sheet by lifting 1 corner of the sheet and pulling it off until completely removed. Place the tray in the dehydrator, and dehydrate at 105°F for 12–18 hours until chips are crispy. Break the chips apart at score lines. Let them cool. Store in a sealed container in a cool, dark place, preferably in a refrigerator or freezer.

Salsa Fresca

Frederic Patenaude's New Year's Day Menu
(www.fredericpatenaude.com)

Prep: 20 minutes
Sit: 1 hour

2 large tomatoes, diced into ¼-inch cubes
½ cup red or white onion, finely chopped and rinsed
2 cloves garlic, minced
½ jalapeño pepper, seeds removed and minced
1 teaspoon lime or lemon juice
½ cup fresh cilantro leaves, chopped
½ teaspoon Celtic sea salt
1 teaspoon apple cider vinegar (optional)

Mix all the ingredients together in a bowl. For the best flavor, allow the salsa to sit for 1 hour at room temperature before serving. Alternatively, pulse all the ingredients in a food processor. Serve with dehydrated corn chips.

Creamy Cucumber Dressing

Karen Ranzi, Creating Healthy Children

Prep: 15 minutes

2 tablespoons pine nuts
1½ cups cucumbers, peeled and chopped
2 stalks celery
2 pitted dates, soaked for ½ hour if not soft
½ lemon, juiced
½ cup fresh dill, chopped

Blend all the ingredients in a high-speed blender. Great as dressing on a leafy green salad.

Goji Coconut Cream Sauce

Eric Rivkin, Give it To Me Raw (www.giveittomeraw.com)

Can be found in Karen Ranzi's book Creating Healthy Children.
Both children and adults love this recipe. This recipe is great as a dressing for salads or as a dip for fruits and vegetables.

Prep: 15 minutes

½ cup Tibetan goji berries, soaked (include soaking water)
½ cup raspberries or blackberries
1 cup young coconut meat
2 dates, pitted
½ teaspoon orange zest (optional)
Enough coconut water to turn over in blender

Blend the ingredients together in a high-speed blender until creamy. Sauce will last up to 3 days in a refrigerator. For an incredibly exotic dessert variation, substitute mango for the raspberries and add 1 banana, ¼ teaspoon of cinnamon, ½ teaspoon of vanilla, and 1 tablespoon of grated ginger. Blend without adding water.

Freaky Fruit Rollups

Jackie Graff, RN, BSN (http://rawfoodrevival.com), rawfoodrevival@att.net

Prep: 15 minutes
Dehydrate: 105°F for 8 hours

4 cups strawberries or any fruit of choice

Place strawberries in a blender until smooth. Pour onto a Teflex sheet and spread evenly. Dehydrate for 8 hours or until completely dry. Peel off the Teflex, cut into pieces, and roll up. Hint: to avoid wasting fruit, especially when too ripe, make roll-ups. Whenever eating sweet, dehydrated fruit or other dehydrated snacks, brush teeth immediately afterward, because the dehydrated fruit is very sweet and acts like pure sugar (we do not want anyone getting cavities from eating healthy).

Caramel Apples
Linda Cooper (a. k. a. Linda Louise Cakes)

Soak: nuts; 4–8 hours
Dehydrate: 4–8 hours until dry
Prep: 45 minutes-1 hour

Apples
1 cup wild jungle peanuts
1 cup pecans
1 cup walnuts
2 Fuji apples
Dash sea salt
Dash cinnamon
Dash nutmeg
½ vanilla bean (scraped)

Caramel
4 tablespoons raw tahini
3 tablespoons pure maple syrup (please note that maple syrup is
        not raw)
4 medium soft dates, pitted
½ teaspoon Celtic sea salt
Dash vanilla (Sun Organic is my favorite)

Apples
Soak, dehydrate, and finely chop the nuts. Mix the nuts in a bowl, add a dash or 2 of sea salt, cinnamon, nutmeg, vanilla bean, and a small amount of maple syrup to lightly coat. Stir by hand to mix well.

Caramel
Process all the ingredients in a food processor until well-blended and smooth. Frost apples with caramel, and then roll in the nut topping, or sit the apples in the middle of the bowl, and press handfuls of nuts into the caramel.

This recipe can be tripled to coat 5 large Fuji apples. You can also melt approximately 1 teaspoon cacao butter to make sure that the caramel sticks on the apples (optional).

I have made just the caramel recipe and served with sliced apples at a party. People either dipped the apples into the caramel or used a small cheese knife to spread caramel on the apples.

Nutty Almond Caramel Apple Slices

Sheryll Chavaria, Raw Can Roll Café and Pure Body Spa,
Douglassville, PA

Raw Can Roll Café in Douglassville, PA, is a new raw restaurant near
me, and this is one of the recipes from owner/chef Sheryll Chavaria.

Soak: nuts; 2–4 hours
Dehydrate: nuts; 4–8 hours
Prep: 30 minutes

3 apples (whichever you desire), cored and sliced, but with peel
　　on (set aside)
1½ cups date paste or 10–16 dates, pitted (room temperature or
　　slightly warm)
1 tablespoons maca (malty flavor)
¾ cup almond milk (see page 182)
½ teaspoon vanilla
Pinch sea salt
Pinch cinnamon
1 cup mashed nuts (any type), set aside (previously soaked and
　　dehydrated)

Combine all the ingredients (except for the apples and nuts) in a
food processor to make the caramel. You may have to open the lid
and scrape down the sides of the food processor to make sure that
everything is mixed well together. Dip the apples into the caramel,
and then into the nuts. Serve.

ALMOND MILK

¾ cup raw almonds, soaked
2–4 cups water

Soak almonds overnight. Rinse the soaked almonds in a colander, and then place in a high-powered blender. Add about 2 cups of water and blend on high speed until smooth and creamy. Pour milk into a milk bag over a container. Use your hands to squeeze the almond mixture until all the liquid is in the container and the bag contains only solid pulp. When I make my almond milk, I also add dates and vanilla during the initial blending process for sweetness (other folks add their flavorings at the end).

Apple Cobbler
Linda Cooper (a. k. a. Linda Louise Cakes)

Linda is one of my long-time potluckers, and she comes up with amazing and spectacular desserts. We have been encouraging her to do more with her talents so, in addition to her and her husband's roofing business (Cooper Roofing), she has started Linda Louise Cakes. If you live in southeast Pennsylvania, you will be able to buy her products locally. If you are not local to us, then she will be able to ship to your home.

Prep: 30–45 minutes
Dehydrate: 4 hours

Cobbler
4 medium apples, cored and peeled (keep 1 separate)
½ soft dates, pitted
½ teaspoon ground cinnamon
1 tablespoon lemon juice
2 tablespoons raw honey or agave
1 teaspoon vanilla
½ teaspoon ground nutmeg
½ teaspoon sea salt

Topping
2 apples, peeled and cored
1 tablespoon raw caramel (see page 179), made with agave
      instead of maple syrup

Cobbler
Combine 1 peeled and cored apple, pitted dates, cinnamon, lemon juice, raw honey, vanilla, nutmeg, and sea salt in a food processor or high-speed blender. Puree until completely soft and creamy. Set aside. Peel, core, and thinly slice the 3 remaining apples. Place

slices in a large bowl and toss with the pureed mix. Place in a medium-sized glass or ceramic dish.

Topping
Combine the peeled and cored apples with 1 tablespoon of raw caramel, spread over the apples, and sprinkle currants on top. Dehydrate for 4 hours at 105°F.

Apple Crisp

Janice Innella, The Beauty Chef

Prep: 45–60 minutes
Dehydrate: 24 hours

Apple Crisp
8 Gala apples, peeled, cored, and sliced
1 cup ground Austria's Finest, Naturally raw pumpkin seeds
2 vanilla beans
Juice of 1 lemon
1 tablespoon cloves, ground
½ teaspoon cardamom seeds, ground
⅛ teaspoon nutmeg
1 teaspoon ginger, ground

Vanilla Sauce
½ cup dates, soaked and pitted
Meat of 1 vanilla bean
1 cup raw cashews

Apple Crisp
You can use the slicer blade in your food processor to slice your apples. Layer apple slices in your pie plate, and sprinkle ground pumpkin seeds on each layer. Combine the remaining ingredients and pour over the apple crisp.

Vanilla Sauce
Blend the above in a high-speed blender. Pour or spread on top of the apple crisp.

Apple Pie

Joel Odhner, Catalyst Cleanse, Rawlife Line, Philadelphia, PA

By now, you have noticed that we have a thing for apples. I live in Pennsylvania, which is a mid-Atlantic state in the United States, and we have apples here all year round (thank God). As you can see, the apple is very diverse.

Prep: 20–30 minutes
Chill: 30 minutes

Crust
2 cups shredded coconut
1 cup dates, pitted

Filling
3 apples, peeled, cored, and sliced
10 dates, pitted
1 teaspoon cinnamon
2 tablespoons psyllium

Crust
Place shredded coconut in a food processor for about 30 seconds. Then add dates and process until sticky. Press into a pie pan.

Filling
Blend all of the filling ingredients in your food processor, and add the psylium last. Process to desired consistency.

Pour the filling into the crust. Chill for ½ an hour and enjoy.

Lasts 3–5 days refrigerated: that is, if you do not eat it all up by then.

It will take you longer to wash the food processor than it will to make this recipe.

Banana Ice Cream

Lisa Montgomery

Peeled bananas, frozen

Freeze peeled bananas, and run through your juicer with a blank blade. The bananas come out like soft-serve ice cream.

Blueberry Cashew Bar

Bruce and Marsha Weinstein, Awesome Foods, Bridgeport, PA (www.awesomefoods.com)

Makes 16 (2 oz.) bars
Prep: 20–30 minutes
Dehydrate: 4 days at 105°F

20½ ounces frozen or fresh blueberries
5 ounces dried blueberries
1 tablespoon cinnamon
1 tablespoon vanilla extract
1/10 teaspoon Himalayan sea salt
21½ ounces raw cashews, finely ground
6 ounces dried blueberries, chopped

Puree the above ingredients, adding the 6 ounces of chopped dried blueberries last. Stir in with a spoon or spatula. On the dehydrator tray, make a 12- by 12-inch square of the mixture and then to cut it into 16 pieces.

Dehydrate at 115°F. On day 2, flip the bars over and turn temperature down to 105°F. Then dehydrate for 2–4 more days. If soft, refrigerate.

All ounces are measured by weight. They are not to be measured in a measuring cup.

Blueberry Cheeseless Cake

Bruce and Marsha Weinstein, Awesome Foods, Bridgeport, PA
(www.awesomefoods.com)

Prep: 30 minutes
Dehydrate: overnight
Makes 8 (4 oz.) slices

Filling

10½ ounces raw cashews

2.8 ounces filtered water

2.3 ounces coconut butter, melted

2.2 ounces agave nectar

1 ounce lemon juice

5.6 ounces fresh or frozen blueberries

¾ teaspoon Himalayan sea salt

1⅓ tablespoons apple pectin

Crust

6.6 ounces almonds, soaked (4.7 ounces dry)

6.6 ounces sunflower seeds, soaked (4 ounces dry)

16.7 ounces Gala apples

0.3 ounce agave nectar

4¾ teaspoons cup cinnamon

¼ teaspoon Himalayan sea salt

¼ teaspoon ginger

1–2 ounces water

Crust

Combine the crust ingredients together in a food processor. Take the dough and mold into a dehydrator tray in a 12- by 12-inch square. Dehydrate overnight. The next day, take the crust, process again with 1–2 ounces of water, and put the crust in a 9-inch pie plate.

Filling
Combine the filling ingredients together in a high-speed blender and pour into the crust. Place in a refrigerator to set.

> All ounces are measured by weight. They are not to be measured in a measuring cup.

Carrot Cake

Joel Odhner, Catalyst Cleanse, Rawlife Line, Philadelphia, PA

Soak: 2–4 hours
Prep: 20–30 minutes

Icing
Soak: 4 hours
Prep: 15 minutes

Cake
2 pounds carrots
2 cups coconut, shredded
2 cups dates, pitted and soaked
¼ cup ginger
1 cup raisins (optional)
2 cups walnuts, soaked and chopped (optional)
1 teaspoon cinnamon
½ teaspoon ground cardamom
1 teaspoon nutmeg
Water, enough to blend

Icing
1 cup cashews, soaked at least 4 hours
2 tablespoons agave nectar
A few drops of alcohol-free vanilla extract
Water for desired consistency

Cake
Place carrots in a food processor and process until fine. Place in a mixing bowl. In a high-speed blender, blend coconut, dates, ginger, and enough water to get it to blend. Transfer the contents into the

carrot pulp bowl. Mix in raisins, walnuts, cinnamon, cardamom, and nutmeg. Press into the pie plate or spring pan.

Icing
Place all the ingredients into a high-speed blender, and blend until smooth. Spread on the carrot cake. Keeps 3–5 days in a refrigerator.

Mindy's Cheesecake

Mindy Marcozzi, Agape Health & Yoga

This is the best cheesecake ever.

Soak: cashews; 1 hour
Prep: 45 minutes
Freeze: overnight

Crust
2 cups raw macadamia nuts
½ cup dates, pitted
¼ cup dried coconut

Cheese Filling
3 cups cashews, soaked for at least 1 hour and chopped
¾ cup lemon juice
¾ cup honey
¾ cup coconut oil
1 teaspoon vanilla
½ teaspoon sea salt (optional)
½ cup water

Raspberry Sauce
1 (16 oz.) bag frozen raspberries
½ cup dates, pitted

Crust
Process the macadamia nuts and pitted dates in the food processor. Sprinkle the dried coconut on the bottom of an 8- or 9-inch spring-form pan. Press the crust onto the coconut. This will prevent sticking.

Cheese Filling

Blend the cashews, lemon juice, honey, gently warmed coconut oil, vanilla, sea salt, and ½ cup of water. In a high-speed blender, blend until smooth and adjust to taste. Pour the mixture onto the crust. Remove air bubbles by tapping the pan on a table. Place in the freezer until firm. Remove the whole cake from the pan while frozen and place on a serving platter. Defrost in the refrigerator.

Raspberry Sauce

Process raspberries and pitted dates in a food processor until well-blended (do not use a blender for this or the raspberry seeds will become like sand). Spread the raspberry sauce over the top of the cheesecake.

Clementine Gelato

Linda Cooper (a. k. a. Linda Louise Cakes)

Prep: 15–20 minutes
Freeze: overnight

2 cups cashews
½ cup coconut butter oil
¼-½ cup agave nectar (depending on sweetness of your
      clementines)
1 teaspoon vanilla extract
1 cup almond milk
1 cup clementine juice
2 teaspoons clementine zest
Pinch of salt

Mix together in a high-speed blender and freeze overnight.

Serve with Snowman Dessert (see page 195).

Snowman Dessert

Linda Cooper (a. k. a. Linda Louise Cakes)

Soak: cashews; 2 hours

Ice Cream
2 cups cashews (soaked)
1 young coconut, meat and water
½ cup almond milk
¼ cup coconut nectar
¼ cup raw honey
¼ teaspoon sea salt
1 whole organic flexible vanilla bean
3 drops vanilla stevia
2 drops Medicine Flower® vanilla flavor extract
1 tablespoon vanilla extract

Moldable Cookie Dough
1 cup cashews (soaked)
½ cup pine nuts
1 cup chopped pear
¼ cup coconut nectar
¼ cup pure Grade B maple syrup
2 teaspoons lemon juice plus 1 (¼-inch) slice lemon with rind
3 drops Medicine Flower® vanilla flavor extract
1 teaspoon sea salt
½ teaspoon nutmeg
¼ teaspoon cinnamon
⅛ teaspoon cardamon
½ cup golden flax meal

Cream Filling
½ cup thick young coconut meat
½ cup cashews (soaked)

½ cup Artisana® organic raw coconut butter (soften in
    dehydrator at 105°F, if needed)
¼ cup coconut nectar
¼ cup raw honey
½ teaspoon sea salt
4 drops Medicine Flower® vanilla flavor extract (or any flavor
    you want)
2 tablespoons coconut water (to blend, if needed)

Ice Cream
Blend all ingredients in a high-speed blender. Pour into 9- by 11-
inch casserole dish with lid and freeze overnight.

Moldable Cookie Dough
Blend all ingredients (except flax meal) in a high-speed blender.
Add blended mixture to flax meal and whisk to incorporate. Spread
batter onto teflex sheets in approximately ⅛-inch thickness. Dry in
dehydrator at 105°F until mixture is dry enough to handle and
reaches a dough-like consistency. Mold into desired shape. For
hard cookies, flip and dry thoroughly, then cut into desired shapes
before batter becomes too dry.

Cream Filling
Blend all ingredients in a food processor until smooth. Refrigerate
to thicken cream, if needed.

Assembly
Make cookie "sandwiches" by filling the hard cookies with cream
or by icing your molded creations with cream. I used the ice cream
as a "snow" base, then sat a molded cookie snowman covered with
cream filling on top of the "snow". Of course, he was also decorated
with a carrot nose, and currants for his eyes and mouth. Be creative
with the arms and scarf.

Fig Christy

Potlucker Christy Parry

Adapted from Janice Inella's recipe in Jill Samter's book, A Complete Guide to Optimal Health: The Road to a Brighter Life.

Prep: 30 minutes
Dehydrate: 24 hours

2 cups black mission figs, soaked to soften (save soaking water)
3 cups pecans, soaked (if desired)
1 tablespoon alcohol-free vanilla
1 tablespoon pumpkin seed oil
1 tablespoon raw honey

In high-speed blender, blend soaked figs and soaking water (use more water, if necessary, to blend until thoroughly mixed).

Place the remaining ingredients in a food processor, adding the fig and water mixture. Process until mixed well.

Spread on a dehydrator sheet to desired thickness, and dehydrate until desired texture (about 24 hours at 112°F).

Mango Cheesecake

Joel Odhner, Catalyst Cleanse, Rawlife Line, Philadelphia, PA

Prep: 20–30 minutes
Serves: 2–3

Filling
1 large mango, really ripe and mushy
1½ cups Brazil nuts
⅛ cup agave or less (if mangoes are really sweet, you may not
        need as much agave; taste first before adding agave, and
        add a little at a time)
½ cup water

Crust
1 cup almond pulp

Filling
Blend all the ingredients until smooth, and set aside.

Crust
In a glass pie plate, cover the bottom with the almond pulp, and
press down to make a crust. If you want your crust to be sweeter,
you can add shredded coconut and pitted dates.

    Spread the filling over the almond pie crust and chill. You can
decorate the top of the cheesecake with strawberries, blueberries,
or goji berries to make a nice presentation.

> When you make almond milk, the left-over pulp is known as
> almond pulp. If you do not want to make almond milk to get to
> the pulp, then grind up the raw almonds with a little water.

Lemon Poppy Seed Flower Cake with Sweet Dehydrated Zucchini Petals

Linda Cooper (a. k. a. Linda Louise Cakes)

Cake
Prep: 30–45 minutes
Freeze: 4–6 hours + 2 hours

Lemon Coconut Frosting
Prep: 15 minutes

Optional Filling
Prep: 15 minutes
Dehydrator: 24 hours +

Cake
2 cups jicama, peeled and cubed
½ cup shredded coconut flakes
1 cup green apple, peeled, seeded, and chopped
3 cups nut pulp (left-over from making nut milk), dehydrated
        and ground to powder
¼ cup flax seeds, ground fine
¾ cup coconut nectar
1 vanilla bean
2 generous teaspoons lemon zest
1 large lemon, juiced
1 tablespoon chia seed, ground
1 tablespoon lucuma
½ teaspoon sea salt
¼ cup poppy seeds (and a bit more for garnish)

Lemon Coconut Frosting
2 cups cashews
1½ whole lemons plus peel, seeds removed

3–4 tablespoons coconut butter

2 drops Medicine Flower vanilla extract

½ cup coconut nectar

3–4 tablespoons water blended with 2 pitted dates

Pinch of sea salt

Optional Filling

Rehydrated dried plums

Dates

Sea salt

Coconut oil

Dehydrated yellow zucchini petals

Honey or agave

Powder mixture of agave powder, lucuma powder, and purple
corn powder

Cake

Place all the ingredients in a food processor, and blend until everything is chopped very fine and moving freely. Press ½ of the mixture
in the bottom of a 9-inch spring-form pan. Smooth the edges and
even the sides as much as possible. Set aside the remainder.

Lemon Coconut Frosting

Place all the ingredients in a high-powered blender. Process until
smooth and fluid.

Frost the bottom layer of the cake, and allow to freeze for 4–
6 hours. Top with the remaining cake mixture and gently press,
again, smoothing the edges and evening the sides. Return to the
freezer for an additional 2 hours. Remove the spring pan, and frost
either the top, sides, or both with the remaining frosting.

I used the frosting on the top and sides of the cake, but added
a plum filling in the middle.

Optional Filling

The filling was a combination of rehydrated dried plums, dates, sea salt, and coconut oil. The petals were dehydrated yellow zucchini, coated with honey or agave. Some were also dipped in a powder mixture of agave powder, lucuma powder, and purple corn powder, and then dehydrated at 105°F until very dry (at least 24 hours).

Love Child Dessert Candy

Potlucker Denise DiJoseph (www.miaura.com)

The "Raw Love Child" tastes of dark chocolate, Raisinets, Mounds, and Almond Joy.

Prep: 30 minutes

1 Haas avocado
¼ cup raisins (or more to taste)
3 heaping tablespoons cacao powder
2 tablespoons (or more to taste) agave or scant-powdered stevia
    (I use Sweet Leaf)
2 tablespoons chia gel
¼ cup (or more to taste) sun-dried or dehydrated flaked
    coconut
½ tablespoon Amazing Grass Chocolate Supergreen Powder
½-1 tablespoon (or more to taste) Health Force Vita Mineral
    Green Powder
Whole raw almonds (presoaked 8 hours and towel dried), to
    garnish

Place the ingredients into a small food processor. If necessary, adjust the recipe by adding more cacao powder or coconut to make a thick dough-like consistency. Use a spring-hinged melon baller, drop portions into miniature fluted muffin papers. Top each candy (optional) with a whole raw almond (presoaked and paper towel-dried). Then if you are already going to use your dehydrator for something else, you can pop these muffin cups into the dehydrator to partially form an outer crust. This is optional, as you can simply eat as is or refrigerate them. Makes about 30 bite-sized portions.

Start with these measurements and adjust according to your taste.
All the ingredients are raw and organic.

Palate Refresher Lemon Sorbet

Janice Innella, The Beauty Chef

Prep: 20–30 minutes
Freeze: 20 minutes

8 lemons (remove skins) or 2 cups lemon juice
3 tablespoons raw honey or agave nectar
1 cup coconut meat or pine nuts
1 teaspoon lemon zest

Blend the sorbet ingredients together well in a high-speed blender. Pour the sorbet mixture into a pre-frozen Cuisinart ice cream maker. It takes approximately 24 hours to freeze your ice cream maker container. It usually takes about 10–15 minutes for the Cuisinart ice cream maker to turn your ingredients into delicious sorbet. Garnish with lemon slices.

Raspberry Sorbet

Mathew Kenney, 105°F Global, LLC

Mathew is the cofounder of 105°F Global, LLC and author of many books such as Everyday Raw *and* Entertaining in the Raw. *I've had the pleasure of taking several of Mathew's classes. The classes and the recipes are always great. This recipe is so easy, quick, and tastes great. In the summertime it is cool and refreshing.*

Prep: 10 minutes

4 cups raspberries
¼ cup agave
½ vanilla bean, scraped
1 cup water or coconut water

Blend all ingredients together in a high-speed blender until smooth.

Strain puree through fine chinois or sieve to remove the seeds.

Process the sorbet base in a Cuisinart Ice Cream Maker and freeze. (It only takes about 10–15 minutes to freeze.) Remember, you have to place your ice cream base in your freezer 24 hours before making the sorbet.

Mango Kiwi Souffle

Sheryll Chavarrria, Raw Can Roll Café, Douglassville, PA

Prep: 30 minutes
Freeze: 20 minutes (or refrigerate for 1 hour)

3 mangoes, deseeded and chopped
2 kiwis, peeled and sliced into rounds
¼ cup agave
½ cup meat of young Thai coconut
Pinch of salt

Blend mangoes, salt, and coconut oil until very creamy. Pour into a big bowl and stir in the kiwi (leave some kiwi slices to top the deserts). Spoon the mixture into individual serving bowls, and top with the rest of the kiwi slices. Place in a freezer for about 20 minutes or in a refrigerator for 1 hour until it sets.

Pumpkin Pulse Cake
Linda Cooper (a. k. a. Linda Louise Cakes)

Makes 10–inch cake
Prep: 30 minutes

Crust
1½ cups organic walnuts
1½ cups organic almonds
1 tablespoon lucuma
¼ teaspoon cinnamon
⅛ teaspoon sea salt
1 teaspoon vanilla
¼ cup raw honey

Filling
3 cups raw organic cashews, hand-shelled and soaked
3 cups organic butternut squash and/or pumpkin, pureed
1 cup almond milk
2 tablespoons lemon juice
1¼ cups agave
1 tablespoon vanilla
⅛ teaspoon sea salt
1½ teaspoons pumpkin spice blend
1 tablespoon sunflower lecithin
1 cup organic coconut oil, melted in dehydrator at 105°F

Crust
Blend in a food processor: mixture forms a ball. Spread onto the bottom of a spring-form pan.

Filling

Blend the first 8 ingredients in a high-speed blender. When smooth, add the last 2 ingredients, and blend well to incorporate.

Pour the filling into a prepared crust, and freeze overnight to set. Thaw for several hours in the refrigerator. Best-served from the fridge. The cake can melt above 76°F. Can be stored for 1–2 months in the freezer, and up to 4 days in the refrigerator.

If you want to eat this pie, but do not feel like making it, please contact Linda at her website, www.lindalouise.org, or call at (610) 476-7653.

Fresh Strawberry Pie

Linda Cooper (a. k. a. Linda Louise Cakes)

Once you try one of Linda's recipes, you will realize why her recipes predominate throughout the desert section of our book. I have known Linda for several years, and her creations are always amazing. I am sharing with you Linda's creations and talent, as they and she are totally outstanding.

Pie Shell
1 cup strawberries, dehydrated
1 cup soft dates, pitted
½ teaspoon vanilla

Binder
7–8 large, ripe strawberries
2 dates, soft and pitted
2 bananas, fairly ripe
1 tablespoon fresh lemon juice

Fruit Filling
2½ pints strawberries, quartered

Crust
Combine the pie-shell ingredients in a food processor or high-speed blender. Press thickly into the pie plate, working from the center to the outside rim to form the shell.

Binder
Blend all the binder ingredients in a food processor or blender until well-mixed.

Fruit Filling

Cut 2 pints of strawberries into quarters, fold into the binder, and fill the shell. Decorate with approximately ½ pint of quartered strawberries.

Cover with plastic wrap, and store in a refrigerator. Chill before serving.

When using the dehydrated strawberry crust, it is not as sturdy as the almond pie crust. Therefore, when using the dehydrated strawberries, you may want to put the filling in a bowl, and crumble the dehydrated strawberry mixture on top.

STURDY PIE CRUST

If you prefer a sturdy crust, please use the following recipe:

Soak: almonds; overnight
Prep: 30–45 minutes
Refrigerate: 4 hours to set

1½ cups almonds
⅓ cup dates
4 tablespoons almond butter
2 cups distilled water
1½ cups sunflower seeds
½ cup fresh coconut

Cover the almonds with distilled water, and soak overnight. Drain. Grate the coconut. Place the almonds and sunflower seeds in a blender or Vitamix®, and process until evenly ground. Add coconut, dates, and almond butter. Mix well. With the machine running, add distilled water by the tablespoon until desired consistency is reached. Press into the pie plate. Refrigerate for 4 hours to set.

MY OWN RECIPES

MY OWN RECIPES

_____

_____

_____

_____

_____

_____

_____

_____

_____

_____

_____

_____

_____

_____

_____

_____

_____

_____

_____

_____

_____

_____

_____

_____

MY OWN RECIPES

_____

_____

_____

_____

_____

_____

_____

_____

_____

_____

_____

_____

_____

_____

_____

_____

_____

_____

_____

_____

_____

MY OWN RECIPES

_____
_____
_____
_____
_____
_____
_____
_____
_____
_____
_____
_____
_____
_____
_____
_____
_____
_____
_____
_____
_____
_____
_____

MY OWN RECIPES

